Testimonials for *Working on a Project Called Life*

You are Chosen! Now, let's move forward.

"Working on a Project called LIFE" is a compelling guide, blending spirituality with practical strategies for fulfilling life's purpose. The author's relatable style and rich experience offer an empowering framework for intentional living, making it an essential tool for those eager to align their actions with their aspirations."

-Susan Friedmann, CSP, international bestselling author of Riches in Niches: How to Make it BIG in a small Market

"This book originates from the author's desire to inspire individuals to embrace and execute their life purpose by integrating project management principles and spirituality. The author incorporates personal experiences into these principles and enhances the narrative with real-life examples, encouraging readers to reflect upon and apply these insights to their circumstances. "Working on a Project Called Life" is a practical guide designed to empower readers in fulfilling their life's purpose."

-Michelle Boodoo, Ph.D. Founder/CEO of In Her Name

"Working on a Project Called Life" was written for a purpose. The author's project management skills and love of our Lord are seen throughout. It is easy to read and contains real-life experiences and reflections. This book will guide and support you as a personalized roadmap to moving forward in your calling and next chapter of life. I pray it will bring awareness to ordinary ladies such as myself. We, too, get stuck and need guidance to move forward in our next chapter of life.

-Maria Carman, Mother, Grandmother, Bible Study Fellowship (BSF) Distance Assistant Online Trainer, Group Leader

In this uplifting read, the author aligns your actions with your divine purpose, transforming abstract concepts into practical tools using project management principles It is a compelling call to action, offering a roadmap ⸀ to fruition. The book's distinctive feature lies in its ⸀ real-life experiences, it becomes a genuine comp⸀ ties. Motivational guidance encourages you to o⸀ purposeful execution.

-Marilyn Hu, President, South Florida Project Management Institute

WORKING

ON A PROJECT CALLED

LIFE

You are Chosen!
Now, let's move forward.

LISA PRATT-SANCHEZ

Working on a Project Called Life

You are Chosen! Now, let's move forward.

Lisa Pratt-Sanchez

ISBN (Print Edition): 979-8-35096-766-1

ISBN (eBook Edition): 979-8-35096-767-8

CONTENTS

DEDICATION

I dedicate this book wholeheartedly to my village—the extraordinary individuals who have been unwavering support throughout my journey. You have listened, believed, and poured your encouragement into the very core of my purpose. Your contribution is immeasurable, and your impact resonates deeply. In every step of this path, you've been more than supporters. You were my cheerleaders, standing on the sidelines, celebrating each milestone, and offering heartfelt applause. Your role as unconditional helpers has taken care of my most fragile and precious purpose assignment. So, to everyone who has shared in this journey, thank you for your human kindness, as your belief in this project has been a constant source of strength. In moments of doubt or challenge, you showed up. Having you in my corner gives me tremendous pride and continues to be a source of motivation and a testament to the power of community. As I dedicate this book to you, I salute your commitment, generosity, and the friendship that binds us together. Here's to you, my village—thank you for having my back and being an integral part of the story these pages tell.

This book extends its embrace to you who have made the courageous decision to embark on the transformative journey of executing your life's purpose. You have chosen to take that decisive step. This is an inspiration for the purpose seekers, the believers, and the doers who are determined to execute their assignment. I also acknowledge and am thankful to the forward-thinking groups/organizations that invest in and support their purpose implementers to reach their full potential. You understand the profound impact of nurturing your team members' growth, well-being, and aspirations. By embracing and investing in the individual, you pave the way for their success and create tangible financial gains and the immeasurable rewards of a supported, valued, motivated, engaged, and fulfilled person. This leads to heightened morale, a positive culture, and a shared sense of purpose that extends far beyond the bottom line.

Ultimately, this book is a testament to the power of individual determination, focus, and drive. It invites you to embark on your journey of self-discovery and fulfillment by pursuing your long-held dreams and answering your unique calling. This book aims to empower and support you as you embrace your calling and provides encouragement and a format to execute your purpose-filled assignments.

FOREWORD / PREFACE

This is a declaration and an invitation to join in a remarkable journey of purpose execution and living. In this book, you will be guided by the author's personal experiences, insights, and the power of embracing one's purpose-driven assignments. It will inspire and challenge you to proceed forward with your calling.

The book highlights the path taken by an individual on a mission. Through her stories and reflections, the author reveals the significance of embracing one's calling and stepping into the fullness of your purpose. This is not a roadmap with all the answers laid out. It is a heartfelt project, a companion guide to your unique journey. It will encourage you to examine yourself and execute your assigned purpose.

Each chapter will remind you of the importance of perseverance in breaking free from self-doubt and rising above the noise to uncover possibilities beyond your reach.

This is an invitation to take steps in navigating your purpose-driven roadmap.

So, are you ready to embark on this adventure?

Are you willing to start your project now and step into the fullness of your purpose?

If so, you are in the right place at the right time.
This book is meant for you.

INTRODUCTION

What is 'Working on a Project Called Life'?

I stated that I would retire at age fifty about twenty-two years ago. I believed it. Over the years, while raising our beautiful and very active children, it became a faint memory. Now, at the fabulous Five-O, I seek more joy and the need to live in and execute my purpose. I was compelled to resign from my job, and as I was planning my next steps, my younger self reminded me of what I had stated years ago. It has been an "AHA" moment. Praises! I am in a new phase of my life, purpose-driven, focused, and happy. I am Working on a Project Called LIFE. The chapters are written as I fill the pages with obedience and personal conviction. I aim to create the opportunity and space for others to walk in their purpose and execute their divine assignments and plans.

While attending a weekend leadership conference with my church a few years ago, I was overwhelmed by all I experienced. This was intended for couples, but I attended alone as this was more my 'cup of tea' than my husband's. There were many profound and introspective discussions followed by personal time for reflection. Something was welling up inside of me, which I didn't want to share with the others. Not knowing what this heavy feeling was, I went to my car for some alone time. I could only seek guidance by reaching for my Bible, where I stumbled upon Proverbs 4, New International Version, "Get Wisdom at Any Cost." The repetition of the word "life" in the verses caught my attention. Additionally, verse 1 of Proverbs emphasizes the importance of listening and gaining intelligent discernment and comprehension, "Listen, my sons, to a father's instruction; pay attention and gain understanding." The words were speaking directly to me, and I felt a rush and desire to do something about it. This very moment was the beginning of my purpose journey for this book.

"Project LIFE" resonated within me, followed by the words **lead, invest, focus**, and **execute**. It was the starting point for discovering how my life purpose could be viewed as a project, ultimately managed with distinct objectives and phases. This was my assignment, and I would utilize my project management skills and background to fulfill it.

Although the encounter at the leadership conference was overwhelming and somewhat frightening, it ignited a sense of curiosity and purpose and a desire to explore the concept of "Project LIFE" further. I now better understand life as a series of random events and a journey that can be approached with intentionality, wisdom, and spiritual discernment. By considering life as a project, individuals can strive to *lead* a strategic journey, intentionally *invest* time and resources, *focus* on their assignments and responsibilities, and *execute* with follow-through and determination.

The concept of Working on a *Project Called LIFE* encourages individuals to actively engage and be deliberate in implementing their purpose.

Project L.I.F.E. – Lead. Invest. Focus. Execute.

➤ **LEAD** with your purpose in mind.

➤ **INVEST** time into understanding your purpose.

➤ **FOCUS** on your purpose calling.

➤ **EXECUTE** as directed on your purpose assignment.

You are to live a life worthy of the calling you have received from the Lord. He calls you to execute His perfect plan for your life, embracing the journey with faith, obedience, and a heart of service. Walking in alignment, you experience the fulfillment, joy, and impact of living out your purpose.

This book provides you with the insight, guidance, and support needed to execute the unique calling in your life. Allow your purpose to guide you as you navigate through your assignment. Stay present in the moment and avoid dwelling on what could have been. Instead of choosing to delay further, you have decided to move forward.

Congratulations, as you are on your way!

Thank you for showing up.

Your project has started.

Stay with me as we work through the process.

Proverbs 4 (NIV)
Get Wisdom at Any Cost

[1] Listen, my sons, to a father's instruction; pay attention and gain understanding.

[2] I give you sound learning, so do not forsake my teaching.

[3] For I too was a son to my father, still tender, and cherished by my mother.

[4] Then he taught me, and he said to me, "Take hold of my words with all your heart; keep my commands, and you will **live**.

[5] Get wisdom, get understanding; do not forget my words or turn away from them.

[6] Do not forsake wisdom, and she will protect you; love her, and she will watch over you.

[7] The beginning of wisdom is this: Get wisdom.
 Though it cost all you have, get understanding.

[8] Cherish her, and she will exalt you; embrace her, and she will honor you.

[9] She will give you a garland to grace your head and present you with a glorious crown."

[10] Listen, my son, accept what I say, and the years of your **life** will be many.

[11] I instruct you in the way of wisdom and lead you along straight paths.

[12] When you walk, your steps will not be hampered; when you run, you will not stumble.

[13] Hold on to instruction, do not let it go; guard it well, for it is your **life**.

[14] Do not set foot on the path of the wicked or walk in the way of evildoers.

[15] Avoid it, do not travel on it; turn from it and go on your way.

[16] For they cannot rest until they do evil; they are robbed of sleep till they make someone stumble.

[17] They eat the bread of wickedness and drink the wine of violence.

[18] The path of the righteous is like the morning sun, shining ever brighter till the full light of day.

[19] But the way of the wicked is like deep darkness; they do not know what makes them stumble.

[20] My son, pay attention to what I say; turn your ear to my words.

[21] Do not let them out of your sight, keep them within your heart;

[22] for they are **life** to those who find them and health to one's whole body.

[23] Above all else, guard your heart, for everything you do flows from it.

[24] Keep your mouth free of perversity; keep corrupt talk far from your lips.

[25] Let your eyes look straight ahead; fix your gaze directly before you.

[26] Give careful thought to the paths for your feet and be steadfast in all your ways.

[27] Do not turn to the right or the left; keep your foot from evil.

Reflection - *River Rafting View*

I am truly honored to be given this assignment. I am called to **live, love**, and **give** freely and continually. This book is a testament to my life, which I genuinely love, and I want to share it with all who need it. Putting action to what you are called to do will enable you to meet the need to deliver. As you faithfully carry out your assignment, you will be transformed into the person you are meant to be. Embrace the growth from the journey, knowing that the process shapes and prepares you for more incredible things. Taking a step is like a leap of faith. I am unsure what the next one will be, but I know I must proceed with this task. The Lord keeps His promises. My future is already written, and I know my purpose needs to be fulfilled. I have been chosen to do this very thing I am now experiencing. It is not for anyone else but for me to bear and demonstrate God's will and love for me.

This book does not define your purpose. It focuses on executing what you have been purposed with and called to do. Use it as your life vest to get on track and better equip yourself to serve others. With consistent use and proper application, you will effectively fulfill your assignment.

Proverbs 4:12 (NIV)

[12] *"When you walk, your step will not be hampered,
and if you run, you will not stumble."*

NOTES & INSIGHTS:

CHAPTER 1:
LIFE is a Project

"There are two great days in a person's life—the day
we are born, and the day we discover why."
WILLIAM BARCLAY, A SCOTTISH AUTHOR, RADIO
AND TV PERSONALITY, MINISTER, AND PROFESSOR OF DIVINITY.

"Project LIFE" emerged during a moment of spiritual reflection and spending time with God. It was revealed that I would utilize my project management skills to fulfill this assignment. From my experiences, I realized that life can be approached and managed like a project with purposeful and intentional actions.

Addressing aspects of your life as projects can bring structure and clarity to your calling. We will look at your purpose as a project to discover insights and principles that can be used to move you forward in your journey. You will be provided with practical tools and strategies for effectively managing the assignments in your life, enabling you to set clear goals, navigate challenges, and achieve meaningful outcomes.

Throughout this journey, you will discover how you can bring intentionality, stewardship, and divine guidance to every goal-oriented project that you undertake. The objective is to equip you with the knowledge and tools to approach the activities in your life as a series of purposeful projects, maximizing your potential and fulfilling your God-given assignments.

Project (*PMI definition*): *According to the Project Management Institute (PMI), a project is a temporary endeavor to create a unique product, service, or result. It is temporary because it has a defined beginning and end in time and, therefore, defined scope and resources. A project is*

*unique because it is not a routine operation but a specific set
of operations designed to accomplish a singular goal.*

Projects and our lives have beginnings and ends, with many activities in between. Life can be viewed as a project requiring intentional steps to imple ment your plan. Effectively managing a project and living your life involves being aware of the tasks at hand, taking ownership of your actions, and considering the impact of your decisions on yourself and those around you.

There will be uncertainties and unexpected challenges along the way. Navigating and adjusting to new situations and circumstances often requires flexibility and adaptability. The ultimate destination or end state may not always be clear, but having a sense of what you want to achieve and the direction you desire to move in is essential.

Setting goals and creating plans can provide you with a sense of clarity and purpose. These plans act as guideposts, helping you make clearer decisions and take actions that align with your desired outcomes. Just as project management principles provide structure and organization, adopting similar approaches in your life can bring order and efficiency.

Breaking down your larger goals into smaller, manageable tasks, prioritizing your activities, and setting timelines can help you make progress and measure your success.

Throughout this Project Called Life, staying connected to your goals and focused on your actions is crucial. Regular self-reflection, seeking wisdom from God, and staying attuned to your inner voice can guide you in making choices that align with your values and purpose. By viewing life as a project and approaching it with purposeful planning and action, you will be better able to navigate its uncertainties, make meaningful progress, and fulfill your purpose with clarity and intentionality.

Living your life with intention goes beyond immediate success; it is about walking in your truth and doing what you are destined to do. Often, we find ourselves surrounded by obligations and tasks that distract us from focusing on what truly matters. However, consciously allocating even a fraction of your time to your assignment can help you progress meaningfully toward your goals. Recognize that the results and rewards may appear in various forms, such as personal growth, joy, peace, and making a difference. Focus on your work's intrinsic value, its impact on others, and the fulfillment it brings to your life. There is usually more to be gained than financial rewards when pursuing your true calling.

As I reflect on my journey, I am grateful for the support and account-ability of my fellow purpose followers. Together, we encourage each other to stay committed. Executing your plan is not always straightforward, as you are constantly pulled in multiple directions. However, you will be more effective when you can prioritize your assignments and dedicate time to them. Inevitably, projects and pursuits can take longer than expected, as we often allow other non-priority tasks to take precedence. Recognizing these distractions and realigning your focus to what truly matters is essential. Writing this book has been a distinct calling that I received years ago, and though it has taken longer than I anticipated, I am determined to complete it and fulfill the specific purpose of writing this book.

My daughter, intending to start a new hobby, gifted me yarn two years ago for Christmas. Due to other activities, it was on the back burner for some time. So when we finally decided to start, I had to search for the tools she had given me. I could not remember where I placed them. I found one of the yarns and even forgot that I had two. I had to be reminded. Eventually, I found the other yarn and the needles. Since this was our first time, we searched and watched a few online tutorials. It took several reviews and many uncomfortable trials to make my first knot and eventually loop over. It was not a natural flow, but each time I did it, I made more progress and better understood the process. The trainers all stated that it would take time to get comfortable finding what works best as the experience was unique to each individual—for example, how to hold the needle. I haven't yet mastered how to grip the needle consistently. But I am excited that I have finally started and felt great accomplishment with my first creation.

There will be steps in your purpose-driven project that will feel unnatural and uncomfortable. Work through it.

Rework it as needed and utilize the tools and resources you have. Like finding and gathering the knitting tools, your journey toward fulfilling your purpose may require searching, discovering, and collecting the necessary resources and support. At the beginning of any new venture, it is expected to feel uncertain and unfamiliar with the steps involved. There may be moments of trial and error, setbacks, and the need to adapt and rework your approach.

Progress can be made with persistence and practice. The same applies to your purpose-driven projects. No matter how small, each step takes you closer to your goal. It is important to embrace the learning process, be patient, and understand that it takes time to become comfortable and find your rhythm. Seek guidance, mentorship, and resources to assist you in your purpose-driven endeavors. There are different approaches and techniques, and seeing what specifically works best for you is essential.

Life is an ongoing journey of self-discovery, perseverance, and prioritization. By embracing your purpose and staying true to yourself, you will make progress and experience the fulfillment that comes from pursuing what you are meant to do. Let us continue to support and inspire one another to live a purpose-filled life and make a positive impact. This can be accomplished by:

- *Working through the uncomfortable and unfamiliar aspects of the assignment.*
- *Embracing the journey.*
- *Adapting as needed.*
- *And utilizing the tools and resources available to you.*

With time, activity, and dedication, you will accomplish the things that align with your assignment. As you become more aware of what you are meant to do, you develop a heightened sense of awareness. As you continue the process, be ready to explore and experience all that comes with it. Be ready to live your purpose-filled life.

Be READY to live your purposed filled life

- Be **Reassured**
- Be **Encouraged**
- Be **Active**
- Be **Determined**
- Be **You**

Be **reassured** in your walk with the Lord, knowing you will be tasked with assignments explicitly meant for you. Stay purposeful as you are designed for this plan beyond your knowledge and understanding.

Be **encouraged**, knowing that you have been hand-picked for the assignment and that the Lord is with you. If He gave it to you, He will see you through it.

Be **active** in seeking the Lord to guide you on your life journey. This will require more than acknowledgment; you must act intentionally on your assignment.

Be **determined** to follow through on your assignment. Make it a priority and move forward as needed.

Be true to **yourself**, as you were called for a reason. You will be used based on your unique set of skills and abilities. You will be given the tools necessary to implement your assignment accordingly. Do not try to be anyone else but yourself in your assignment.

As we work on your project, this **framework** will be used and referenced throughout the book to execute your purpose.

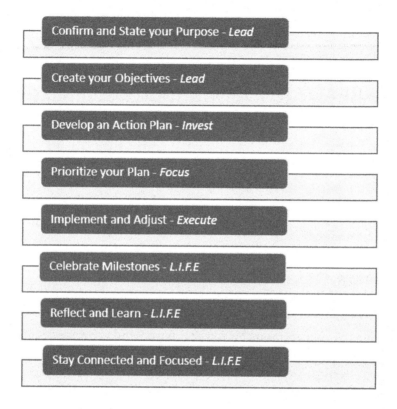

Confirm and State your Purpose - *Lead*

Create your Objectives - *Lead*

Develop an Action Plan - *Invest*

Prioritize your Plan - *Focus*

Implement and Adjust - *Execute*

Celebrate Milestones - *L.I.F.E*

Reflect and Learn - *L.I.F.E*

Stay Connected and Focused - *L.I.F.E*

The format allows you to break down your purpose into actionable steps, track your progress, and adjust as needed. It provides a structured approach for execution and helps you stay focused and aligned with your goals. We will discuss each section in more detail, customize the sections to fit your specific assignment, and adjust them as necessary throughout your project.

Reflection - **Vision Board View**

(Created months before any knowledge of my diagnosis)

The recent news I received of a pituitary brain tumor has brought forth a wave of uncertainty and apprehension. Yet, in the midst of it all, there is a steadfast faith that propels me forward to continue this assignment.

With each step I take, I am acutely aware of the need to embrace this new chapter of my life with courage and resilience. It would be easy to succumb to fear and allow it to paralyze me, but that is not my chosen path. Instead, I see this as an opportunity to live in my purpose.

More tests, consultations with specialists, and even difficult decisions will occur. But I am not defined by this diagnosis; I am defined by my unwavering spirit and belief that I am on a purposeful journey. This is a single aspect of my life, serving as a reminder that even in the face of adversity, I can rise above and embrace the challenges that come my way. My purpose remains unchanged, and if anything, this newfound knowledge only fuels my determination to make a difference in the lives of others.

I am writing these words with an understanding that this detour does not hinder my plans. They may take a different shape and require different actions, but the essence of my assignment remains intact. Through this experience, I pray to learn more about myself and gain the wisdom and empathy needed to touch the lives of others facing their battles.

I am armed with faith, hope, and trust in the Lord. I plan to face each day with renewed purpose, knowing I am not alone. This journey, though challenging, will continue to shape and mold me. I hold on to the belief that I am not defined by my circumstances but rather by my commitment to live a life of purpose, on purpose. Although the plans may shift, and the timeline may change, I am determined to embrace this chapter and continue moving forward, trusting that there is a greater plan unfolding, one that will reveal itself in due time. In this truth, I find strength and the assurance that I am exactly where I need to be.

Proverbs 4:20 - 22 (NIV)

[20] *My son, pay attention to what I say; turn your ear to my words.*

[21] *Do not let them out of your sight; keep them within your heart;*

[22] *for they are **life** to those who find them,*
and health to one's whole body.

NOTES & INSIGHTS:

CHAPTER 2 LEAD:
"Take the Leap"

Chosen

Natural,

Forced,

Or by circumstance?

However,

Whenever,

You've been chosen

To lead paths unknown

Sights unseen

Could it be?

Why me?

Chosen…

Lisa P-S

Everyone has a purpose and is meant to lead in it. Although the why may not always be clear, know that you are chosen for a specific calling. When chosen, you will likely need to *modify* your behavior to *edify* others and *magnify* your calling while *glorifying* His name.

The act of being chosen gives a sense of duty and purpose. It is a commitment that will require your energy and time. It usually involves personal improvement and a selfless dedication with a broader reach and impact to enhance the well-being of others. You are edifying others by focusing on positive changes and fostering an environment where individuals can thrive and reach their full potential. This is a transformative journey with a broader focus to magnify your calling. You are expected to amplify its impact, ensuring its significance resonates deeper and more significant. Your spiritual connection to the assignment will further deepen and align your actions with principles that are ordained for you.

LEAD with your purpose in mind.

Lead (Merriam-Webster definition): *To direct the operations, activity, or performance.*

Be the Leader you are called to be in your assignment. Take hold of what has been given to you; to foster, care for, and develop. Bring to life the very thing meant for you, even before you knew it. It has been given to you with authority, from authority. You have the power, the privilege, and the right to take command of your purpose. Though it may require assistance from others, you are the main driver and leader in the effort.

Your purpose was formed because of you and assigned to you.

When I first received the assignment to write this book at the conference, my immediate reaction was a powerful urge to escape. I felt a surge of fear, prompting me to take decisive action. In a moment of distress, I sought refuge in the solace of my car, wanting to be alone as I desperately hoped the overwhelming emotions would go away. Sharing this unwelcome feeling with the others attending the conference seemed daunting, even unbearable. I yearned for the familiar comforts of home, where I felt safe and secure, where life followed its somewhat ordinary, predictable course and routines.

The fear of the unknown or of exposing vulnerability can trigger your impulse to escape or avoid discomfort. The desire to return to the familiar is a natural reaction when facing something new. Acknowledging and recognizing these feelings is important in understanding and addressing them. It's okay to feel overwhelmed and fearful when confronted with unfamiliar challenges. Processing these emotions may take time, and you can gradually step into the challenge at your desired pace.

Your purpose is your unexpected miracle
waiting to be brought into existence.

It often resides outside your abilities, expecting to stretch you beyond your perceived limits to manifest its extraordinary potential. Dare to step outside your comfort zone, where growth and opportunity reside. Dream bigger and take bold actions to turn those dreams into reality.

Purpose leaders are chosen and appointed. Being the leader of the things you are positioned for encourages you to live out your purpose and positively impact those around you. You can grow into the individual you are called to be and lead a life that brings glory to God. Leaders should stand firm in their calling and trust the Lord for guidance. By doing so, they learn how to navigate the challenges and trials of life to accomplish their assignment.

As you assess your calling, think and reflect on the following:

1. Do you know or understand your purpose(s)?

2. Is there something that you consider too big or beyond your reach?

3. What are you hesitant to start due to feeling unprepared?

4. Are you uncertain about taking the next steps in your purpose?

5. Are you questioning the Lord if you are the right person?

6. Is this pushing you out of your comfort zone and making you uneasy?

The insights from your assessment and reflection may be the assignment that you are meant to lead.

God uniquely creates you for the good works He has prepared for you. By seeking His will, surrendering to His guidance, and stepping into the assignments He has for you, you can live a life that honors Him and blesses those around you.

From defining tasks and action items to identifying people and available resources to assessing potential roadblocks and moving forward, you will gain practical tools to lead your project confidently. Even the most straightforward assignments can be transformed into powerful and effective projects when approached with intention and clarity.

> *When you are chosen, the impractical becomes practical, the impossible becomes possible, and the illogical becomes logical.*

Accepting said assignment will remove obstacles and strengthen your faith and ability to accomplish your purpose.

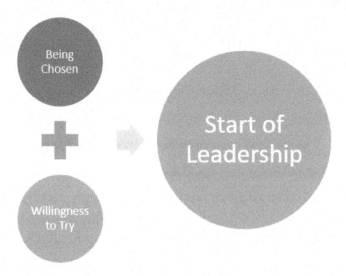

The first step in the process is to acknowledge your assignment. Embracing the leadership role is crucial, so saying yes to the project is important. You should say yes without any conditions and allow the process to guide you. Not "Yes, but what if," or "Yes, when I can," just YES. When I first received my assignment, my focus was that it would be okay if only I were a writer. So much time passed based on my "ifs." Now that I have fully accepted my assignment, I have changed my "if only" to "I know" and "I believe" that I am a writer. This is not because I have gotten a physical document or certification; I have been spiritually qualified and reminded of my many gifts. I write because I believe, and based on that belief, I write.

Accepting your assignment wholeheartedly demonstrates a willingness to trust in, adhere to, and rely on God's plan for your life. You now open yourself up to the opportunities and lessons that come with it. It allows you to let go of rigid expectations and adapt to the changing circumstances that may arise during the journey.

Projects have a goal or an outcome in mind, but the steps to get there will likely vary with unexpected twists and turns. Accept and be comfortable, knowing that the end goal will be what it needs to be, even if the path is unclear. It's important to embrace the uncertainties and challenges that may arise along the way. Your project's ultimate fulfillment will give you a deeper meaning and understanding of who you are and what you are meant to do. Embrace the journey with faith, resilience, and an unwavering commitment to fulfilling your purpose, trusting that it will manifest how it needs to.

When you align with God's plan, He will provide the tools, people, and opportunities to carry out the work.

You need to accept the assignment without placing any conditions. Anything other than a definitive response will delay the work that needs to be done, and you risk disconnecting from His plan and missing out on the fullness of His glory in your life. This will result in you being out of sync with your purpose. Leading your assignment requires you to step out in faith and embrace the unknown, most likely. In taking that leap, you must entrust your assignments to God's guidance, knowing He will provide the necessary wisdom and strength.

In my initial writing journey, I attended a writer's conference due to my conversation with my sister regarding my purpose assignment. I then had tools available to me to start the process. It is now years later due to my disobedience and neglect, but thankfully, I am now part of a writer's group based on another conversation I had with my executive coach. In that group, I am exposed to additional resources, such as a speaking forum, where I have been able to hone my skills further and build my network. This is all possible because I am finally focused and wholeheartedly said yes to writing this book.

<u>Purpose Acknowledgement and Acceptance</u>

- *Recognize your purpose and divine design.*

  o Understand that you have been chosen and tagged for a specific purpose. Though it may feel daunting and overwhelming, acknowledge that you have been selected for this journey.

- *Embrace your calling.*

  o Shift your thoughts from fear and resistance to acceptance and gratitude. Even though it may appear scary and uncertain, consider yourself fortunate to have been entrusted with this unique assignment. Understand that it is not within your strength or control but through His grace that you have been chosen.

- *Emphasize obedience and responsibility.*

  o Recognize that it is not merely a matter of personal will or preference but a must-do based on your calling. By realizing the importance of carrying out your assignment, you understand that fulfilling what has been entrusted to you is essential.
  o Acknowledge the significance of your role and consider the consequences of leaving the assignment undone.

Embarking on your purpose journey can evoke excitement, fear, uncertainty, and even resistance. Having mixed emotions is normal as you enter the unknown and face unexpected challenges. In these moments, it can be helpful to remember that the *assignments and purpose given to you are unique to your strengths, passions, and calling.* While it may feel daunting, you can find comfort knowing that you have been chosen and entrusted with this task for a reason.

Embrace the unknown and trust that you have what it takes to fulfill your purpose. Stay open to learning, be willing to step outside your comfort zone, and celebrate the progress and growth along the way. Your journey is unique, and your experiences will shape and mold you into the person you are meant to be.

Taking the leap of faith in your purpose also requires you to be somewhat adventurous, possibly embracing different ways of doing things and taking bold actions in alignment with God's plan for your life. Trust the Lord to remove any doubt or fear as He guides you and makes it possible to step into your rightful position for your assignment. Your ability to pray, seek wise counsel, and align with your inner being allows you to make confident choices and navigate leadership challenges.

Let's start on your assignment, assuming you have identified your purpose and are ready for the next step.

1st Phase: Purpose Initiation

The Purpose Initiation phase is the first phase of your project cycle. It is where you will assess your purpose and convert it into meaningful steps. Your purpose assignment is the overall goal and objective. Now that it has been identified, it is time to break it into smaller components.

Transitioning into this phase requires understanding your assignment and articulating your purpose, values, passions, and what brings you fulfillment. This clarity will guide your actions and decision-making in executing your project.

The goal is to develop a purpose plan outlining the tasks, resources, and timelines required to accomplish your assignment. Breaking your purpose assignment into smaller, manageable tasks can make tracking progress less overwhelming and more straightforward. To build the plan, you must identify the goal. Refer to the Purpose Statement - Template 1 in the Appendix.

Purpose Statement - Template 1

Item	Insight	Input
Clarity of purpose		
	Assess how well you understand your purpose or the specific impact you want to make.	Ex. I am tasked with writing a book on purpose execution.
	Reflect on whether your purpose is clearly defined and can be articulated concisely.	Ex. Although I am not clear about the audience, I know this is meant for individuals uncertain of how to move forward with their next steps.
Assignment		
	Identify areas where you feel a sense of calling or responsibility.	Ex. Purpose assessment & execution, project management, leadership, people
	Consider any specific assignments or tasks you believe you have been called or destined to fulfill.	Ex. Writing, Speaking, Mentoring others, Volunteering

PURPOSE STATEMENT

Write a clear and concise statement that represents your purpose or specific goal

(At this time, how would you describe the primary purpose and focus of your assignment?)

Purpose Statement example:

I am called and purposeful in writing a book on executing my God-given life assignments, leveraging my skills and background as a project manager.

To further fine tune your goals and objectives, refer to the Purpose Assessment Checklist - Template 2 in the Appendix.

Purpose Assessment Checklist - Template 2

Item	Insight	Input
✓ **Purpose goals & objectives**		
	Set clear goals and define your objectives.	*Ex. Write a book on purpose execution.*
	Break goals down into smaller, manageable tasks and action-able steps.	*Ex. Focus on the book title and table of contents.*
	This activity aims to make the process less overwhelming and enable you to see progress along the way.	
	A clear roadmap will help you stay focused and motivated.	

✓ List To-do's that go beyond day-to-day tasks		
	Identify tasks or activities that align with your long & short-term goals and that support your purpose.	*Find books, writers, and groups that can provide insight into the writing process.*
	Include actions contributing to personal growth, fulfillment, and making a difference.	*Join a writing group.*
✓ List items that appear bigger than you or beyond your reach		
	List goals or dreams that may initially seem challenging or ambitious.	*Ex. Create a book proposal and attend a writing conference.*
	Consider opportunities that require stepping out of your comfort zone.	*Ex. Schedule meetings with book publishers at the conference.*
✓ List what others may have seen in you that you haven't seen		
	Reflect on feedback or observations from others regarding your strengths, talents, and potential.	*Ex. Family and friends showed excitement about the book, stating that I have great insights and continually provided encouragement.*
	Take note of qualities or abilities that people have recognized in you, but you may not have fully acknowledged.	*Ex. Ability to tell a story, speaking with passion and conviction, personable, driven*

✓ What do you spend most of your time on		
	Evaluate where you invest the majority of your time and energy.	Ex. work, volunteering, family, friends
	Determine if these activities align with your core values and long-term aspirations.	Ex. I need to find a hobby just for me. I enjoy connecting with people. How can I do that more effectively?
	Identify areas where you feel a sense of calling or responsibility.	Ex. Helping others in need.

Using this purpose assessment checklist allows you to evaluate different aspects of your life and gain further insights into your purpose. It helps you identify areas of focus, potential growth opportunities, and areas you may need to adjust to align with your purpose. Remember that this checklist is meant to guide your self-reflection and is customizable to your unique circumstances and aspirations.

As a leader, you will discover how to turn everyday tasks into purposeful projects and embark on a journey of purpose fulfillment. You will be equipped with the knowledge and inspiration to assess your assignments, set clear goals, and confidently leap into your God-given purpose. Initiating your purpose plan requires determination, resilience, and a willingness to embrace the unknown. Stay committed to your vision, stay connected to your why, and keep learning and growing. Your purpose has the potential to make a meaningful impact, and by taking intentional steps, you can bring it to life. Often, the hardest part is taking the first step. Overcome any hesitation or fear by getting started. Remember that progress is made through consistent action.

When you feel like you are alone, with nobody understanding or acknowledging the ordained nature of your assignment, it can be a challenging and isolating experience. It may seem this calling can be wished away, talked out of, reassigned, or ignored. In such moments, it is important to remember that you are not alone and God is with you. You should know that there is strength and purpose in your unique position. Find reassurance in your faith, rely on your inner guidance, and trust that you have been chosen for a reason. Your obedience and commitment to fulfilling your calling will have a meaningful impact, even if the finish line is not yet in sight.

Throughout the process, seek guidance and trust your intuition continually. Pay attention to your gut feelings. Your inner voice may caution you to divert or move away from certain paths. Trust that discernment and follow your instincts. Remember that life is constantly changing, requiring us to flow and adapt. While concerns may still arise, they will no longer deter you because you have been chosen to see this through.

Strategies to Cultivate Leadership Skills

- **Stay** focused and motivated by regularly reminding yourself of your purpose and the impact it will have.

- **Surround** yourself with positive influences, inspiration, and accountability partners who can support and encourage you. Share your goals and aspirations with them and ask them to hold you accountable. Their reminders and support can help you stay on track and overcome challenges.

- **Seek** out self-improvement opportunities to build your character and credibility by focusing on the things within your control. Recognize that you can change the course of negative self-talk and disappointments. By staying committed to your purpose and taking intentional actions, you can overcome obstacles and create positive change in the lives of those you serve.

- **Stay steadfast** in your faith, trust the Lord's plan, and continue pursuing your purpose-driven life. The journey may have its challenges, but with God's guidance and unwavering dedication, you will make a lasting difference in those you touch.

Side note: *Leaders are not perfect; they are people who continually work to be better for themselves and others.*

Our leadership skills start and are cultivated at a young age. Have you ever played the children's game tag? In tag, when you are tapped, you take on the role of the "tagger" and must actively seek out your targets. The game requires active movement, strategy, and quick thinking. The dynamics of the game mirror aspects of leadership and goal pursuit. I equate TAG to Transformation and Growth. As the tagger, you effectively become the leader with the mission to achieve the specific goal. This involves agility, awareness, and the ability to focus to complete the assignment. It's not just about physical speed but also mental awareness and adaptability. The game encourages a sense of responsibility and a willingness to take on an active role. Once tagged, the new "It" assumes the lead position and carries the game forward. This represents being targeted, taking charge, and teamwork to achieve an end goal.

The ability to transform into a leader, set objectives, and actively work towards achieving them is a fundamental skill that can be applied in many areas of life. A leader is most effective not just by holding a position of authority but also by being committed to serving others and actively providing assistance. They can adjust when necessary.

When working with my team during high-stress moments, I would remind them that this, too, shall pass. I sometimes state that it was not as serious as performing brain surgery to refocus the team, normalizing the severity to get back on track. I didn't realize that those words would come back to me when I had to undergo brain surgery of my own. I prayed about the procedure, more importantly, the doctors who had to perform the surgery. I then realized how important our gifts are and how reliant others can be on such services. Your faith truly gets tested when you are in the midst of your storm. You cannot do this life alone, as we are connected through our experiences and our beliefs. I trust you handle your assignment carefully, as it is just as delicate as any other.

You have been given the authority to lead and entrusted with the gifts to execute your purpose, which is meant for you to fulfill.

Jeremiah 1: 5-7 (NIV)

[5] *"Before I formed you in the womb I knew you, before you were born I set you apart; I appointed you as a prophet to the nations."* [6] *"Alas, Sovereign Lord," I said, "I do not know how to speak; I am too young."* [7] *But the Lord said to me, "Do not say, 'I am too young.' You must go to everyone I send you to and say whatever I command you.*

Reflection - _Clear Beach Day View_

Helping people by being there for others is a big part of my purpose. It comes up naturally in my personal and professional experiences. Although broad, it is more specifically related to giving back my time, resources, and talent. While still a work in progress, I am grateful for the assignment. I embraced that the Lord assigned me a special and unique plan. I feel blessed to know that He has a plan for me. His continued belief in me is a testament to my worth and the potential impact I can have in the lives of others. I accept this assignment with gratitude and grace, knowing I am a part of something greater than myself.

He hasn't given up on me; therefore, I need to keep the assignment in motion, chipping away at it, one task at a time. I will focus on the things within my control and pray for guidance on the follow-through.

"I am assigned to assist and support individuals motivated by their purpose to live their lives intentionally and without apology by purposefully executing their goals."

This encapsulates my mission and serves as a guiding principle for my actions. I keep it at the forefront of my mind as a reminder of my commitment to others and the meaningful impact I make for a greater purpose. The work is plenty; we are all expected to do our part. I stand with you today in your journey to face your assignment and celebrate your conscious decision to move forward in the right mindset. Thank you, Lord. You are mighty and worthy to be obeyed and praised. Amen.

Proverbs 4:13 _(NIV)_

[13] _Keep hold of instruction; do not let go; guard her, for she is your **life**._

NOTES & INSIGHTS:

CHAPTER 3 INVEST:
"Set the Stage"

Invest (Merriam-Webster definition): *To make use of, for future benefits or advantages.*

Investing your time means intentionally allocating your resources and energy. It involves looking beyond your needs and desires to accomplish what needs to be done. You are encouraged to put your time and attention into what has been entrusted to you and limit being wasteful in service to yourself and others.

Reflect on what you spend your time on. Investing your time requires effort.

1. What is occupying most of your time?

2. How have you prioritized what you spend your time on?

3. How are you maximizing the pockets of time you have?

4. What currently demands your time, both from yourself and others?

5. What have you done for someone else recently?

6. Are you actively engaged in your tasks?

7. With whom are you spending your time?

8. Do you feel you've been selfless and made sacrifices with your time?

9. Do you view your time as a valuable investment?

10. What adjustments could you make in your routine to optimize your time?

Ultimately, investing your time in the things meant for you to do further enriches your life and, conversely, blesses those around you.

It deepens your sense of purpose, strengthens your relationships, and brings you closer to your calling.

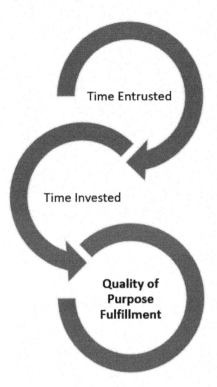

Just as a project requires careful planning and preparation, so does your journey and the time spent towards fulfilling your purpose. It is important to continually seek God's wisdom and guidance in every step, aligning your plans with His purpose for your life.

We will outline practical strategies and techniques to help you plan and organize your project effectively. *From defining clear objectives, identifying key milestones, creating a timeline, and assigning resources*, you will gain valuable insights into structuring your journey toward purposeful living. We will address potential challenges and roadblocks during the planning phase, providing strategies to overcome them and stay focused on your goals. We will emphasize the importance of flexibility and adaptability, recognizing that plans may need to be adjusted as you gain new insights and experiences.

Therefore, this chapter will help you grasp the planning phase and provide practical tools for effectively allocating time for your life project assignment. You will be empowered to create a plan that aligns with your purpose. The success of your project hinges on effective planning, implementation, and having the proper support and sponsorship in place.

> **Project Sponsorship** (PMI definition): *Project sponsor(s) typically are members of senior management who carry a respectable level of influence and authority and serve as proponents of projects.*

You will gain the divine support needed when you walk in your purpose. Since your purpose was God-given and ordained by Him, He walks with you along the way, playing roles such as your guide, investor, board member, teammate, and supporter. The Lord is your ultimate Sponsor. He assigned you your purpose and will support and guide you. Like a project sponsor in business, the Lord takes ownership of your project and supplies all the necessary resources for its success. This is reassuring as He is all-knowing, all-powerful, and ever-present. His wisdom, strength, and love are always available to you. He knows the intricacies of your purpose and understands what is required for its fulfillment. With Him as your Sponsor, you can have confidence that you are not alone in this endeavor.

He will equip you with the required talents, gifts, and opportunities. He will open doors and make a way where there seem to be limitations or no way forward. When you encounter challenges or obstacles, He will guide you and provide you with the ability to resolve and overcome them. The Lord's sponsorship extends beyond mere provision. He cares deeply about your project and its impact. He is invested in your success and desires to see you thrive. His support is unwavering, and His commitment to your purpose is unyielding.

The Lord is our guiding light. He shadows us even when He cannot be seen. Similar to our shadow in the natural, if you are walking to the light, your shadow follows you. Additionally, your shadow, although faded, is with you even when walking away from the light. It is impossible to get rid of our shadow, seen or unseen. Knowing that the Lord is your Sponsor should bring great comfort. He is your unwavering companion on your journey. You can trust His faithfulness, lean on His strength, and rely on His guidance. With Him by your side, there is no limit to what you can achieve in fulfilling your purpose.

Take confidence in the fact that your project has the ultimate sponsor—the Lord Himself. He is with you every step of the way, providing the resources, support, and guidance needed for your success. Embrace His sponsorship, and let it fuel your determination and inspire your actions.

2nd Phase: Purpose Planning

CREATE AN ACTION PLAN WITH A PURPOSE

BUILD SOLID RELATIONSHIPS ON PURPOSE

MANAGE YOUR TIME PURPOSEFULLY

GIVE BACK FOR A GREATER PURPOSE

 ## Create An Action Plan with a Purpose

You will develop a plan and strategy that outlines the steps and actions required to launch your purpose and achieve your goals. Setting clear goals and creating a plan will provide structure and direction. The detailed plan identifies the tasks, associated timelines, and the necessary resources for your assignment. You must break down your more extensive purpose assignment into smaller, actionable steps. The tasks must be manageable and prioritized for tracking purposes. This will allow you to assess progress and celebrate milestones along the way. Unlike a standard project, your purpose plan may have more unknowns than specific steps, which is expected. This is new for you, and you must discern the proper steps to take throughout the process. As a result, it is ok to have some undefined or generic tasks. Give yourself grace in the process. Your plan is a living document that can be revised and updated.

- **Primary Planning Considerations**

o *Refine Tasks and Activities*

From the goals identified in the previous chapter, you will refine the plan by creating SMART goals. Each task should be specific, measurable, attainable, relevant, and time-bound, aligning with your purpose. You will also set meaningful milestones by breaking down your purpose and identifying checkpoints. These milestones will serve as progress markers and help you stay motivated and encouraged as you move forward.

o *Assign Resources*

Remember that you are not alone on this journey. Surrounding yourself with people who understand and support your purpose can make a significant difference in staying motivated and overcoming challenges.

- Identify your team and the resources needed to accomplish your purpose.

- Assess who you already have and the additional resources you may need.

- Take stock of available resources, including your knowledge, experiences, networks, and physical assets. This may include financial resources, equipment, skills, and a support network.

- As needed, create an approach for getting the necessary resources or enhancing existing ones. Consider seeking support from mentors, accountability partners, and a community of like-minded individuals who can offer guidance, encouragement, and a listening ear.

Refer to the Resource Roster - Template 3 in the Appendix: Resource Name → Type → Contribution → Commitment → Status.

Resource Roster - **Template 3**

Resource Name	Type	Contribution	Commitment	Status

Resource Roster Example

Resource Name	Type	Contribution	Commitment	Status
Writing Subscription	Website	Training	Yearly, participate in writing topics, challenges	*Active*
Writing Group	Support	Writing	2x weekly for an hour	*Active*
Books	Reading	Information on writing	Research and read materials on non-fiction writing	*Continual*
Professional Individual	Personal Coach	Personal plan	Include as part of my plan to make myself accountable	*In Progress*
Bible Study Fellowship (BSF)	Women's study group	Spiritual support	Participate in ongoing studies for biblical truths and support	*Active*

o *Define time blocks*

Identify the effort it will take and utilize time management techniques to prioritize your tasks and allocate dedicated time for working on your purpose.

Start with larger time blocks for the unknown and revise as needed. Refer to the Purpose Plan - Template 4 in the Appendix: Activity / Task → Resource → Timeframe → Duration → Status.

Purpose Plan - Template 4

Activity / Task	Resource	Timeframe (Start / End Date)	Duration (i.e. Days, Weeks, Months)	Status (Not started, In Progress, Complete)

As you are destined to lead in this assignment, you will find that you are involved in many of the tasks as a valuable resource. It is necessary to pray for guidance and seek help from others. It is understood that the Lord is your Sponsor and is with you every step of the way. Therefore, you can list Him in your task list where you feel most compelled.

Purpose Plan Example

Below is a high-level plan I created when I first began this journey. I pray it provides you with some insights into making your unique plan.

Activity / Task (Start with an action)	Resource	Timeframe (Start / End Date)	Duration (i.e. Days, Weeks, Months)	Status (Not started, In Progress, Complete)
Write the book	Self	TBD	1 – 3 Years	Not Started
Identify the title	Self	TBD	2 Weeks	In Progress
Fine-tune the title	Self	TBD	Ongoing	Not Started
Research how to be a writer	Self, friends with published books, online research	TBD	1 Month	Not Started
Pray & and ask for guidance	Self, bible study group	TBD	Daily	In Progress
Prepare content outline	Self, Advisor	TBD	2 Months	Not Started
Milestone: 1st draft of book title and content outline completed	Self	TBD		Not Started
Determine Audience	Self, Sponsor (God)	TBD	Ongoing	Not Started
Research the Book creation process	Self, Online, Conferences, Other Writers	TBD	Ongoing	Not Started
Seek out / Join Groups /support system	Self, Writing groups/clubs/organizations	TBD	Ongoing	Not Started
Milestone: Gained more insights into book writing and sought out support	Self	TBD		Not Started
Write each chapter	Self	TBD	Ongoing	Not Started
Milestone: Chapter X completed	Self	TBD		Not started
Review and edit the chapters	Self, Editor(s)	TBD	Ongoing	Not Started
Publish the book	Self, Book Publisher	TBD	Ongoing	Not Started
Final Milestone: Book is written and complete	Self, Sponsor	TBD		Not Started

• Additional Planning Considerations

Identify the associated risks, personal fears, concerns, and potential road-blocks you may encounter in your assignment.

Risk (PMI definition): An uncertain event or condition that, if it occurs, has a positive or negative effect on a project's objective.

- Identify any risks, gaps, or challenges that may impact the execution of your purpose.

- You must determine how you will address these risks and concerns.

- Anticipate possible setbacks and mentally and emotionally prepare to navigate them.

- Build a backup plan to address the risks and overcome challenges.

  o **Potential risks/fears**: other priorities, distraction, giving up, self-sabotage / negative self-talk, non-supporters, naysayers, freedom of your time, environment, health, finances, experiences, and disappointments. Recognize the presence of your inner critic. Be aware of the thoughts and beliefs that hold you back or create doubt. By acknowledging these inner obstacles, you can start working to overcome them.

  o ***Backup Plan*** (*action to be taken if risk occurs*): Give yourself grace, pray about it, seek advice from a support network, refine tasks and schedule, review what you learned, etc.

  o ***Document***: Write down the risks, fears, and concerns related to your assignment. This exercise helps bring them to light and allows you to evaluate them objectively. Develop strategies to deal with these risks and consider potential solutions in advance.

See the example below and refer to the Risk Review Register - Template 5 in the Appendix: Risk Description → Impact → Action to address → Owner

Risk Review Register – Template 5

Risk Description	Action to Resolve	Owner

Risk Review Register Example

Risk Description	Action to Resolve	Owner
Time Management – finding the time to write	Seek out pockets of time to focus on writing. Spend less time watching TV and on social media.	Self
Prioritization – ensure this is included with the other tasks that I am expected to complete	Include weekly checklist items on my calendar to prevent delays and forgetting about the task.	Self
Fear of letting others know	Start sharing with close family and friends who can provide encouragement and support.	Self

- o **Identify potential costs**

  - Assess the costs for each task in your Purpose Plan.
  - Financials, time constraints, your relationships, etc. *Side note*: Relationships may improve or become obsolete.

- o **Create a Communication Checklist**

  - How and what will you communicate, and to whom?
  - Communication is vital and will keep your purpose in motion.

See the example below and refer to the Communication Checklist - Template 6 in the Appendix: Communication Type → Purpose *(what to communicate)* → Target *(who to communicate to)*

Communication Checklist – Template 6

Communication Type	Purpose	Target

Communication Checklist Example

Communication Type	Purpose	Target
Word of Mouth	Whenever led, share my purpose project. It comes up in conversation as the spirit leads me.	Those that I am in conversation with. Friends, Family, Co-workers, Strangers
Email	Send emails to potential endorsers or supporters. Participate in online groups to learn and share your project.	Other writers (first-time and seasoned); support groups with similar purposes for idea sharing
Text	Reach out and connect by sharing a word and insight on my progress.	Accountability crew and support groups.
Prayer	Continue to ask the Lord for guidance and support on the purpose assignment.	My Lord and Savior.
Social Media	As led, share what is on my heart. This is a form of giving back and provides insight into continuing on my journey.	My social network and support group.

Build Solid Relationships on Purpose

Implementing your purpose can become overwhelming; it is vital to cultivate meaningful relationships with others. This will provide you with support, guidance, and collaboration opportunities. As you gain a clearer insight into your assignment, you will also gain a better perspective on your circle of influence. The people assisting you with your purpose could be a part of the audience that will achieve the biggest impact from your follow-through and implementation. These individuals could have also been purposed to assist you and await the invitation. Ensure that you allocate dedicated time for your tasks while also making time for interactions with others. Prioritize your work by setting boundaries and managing your time effectively to stay focused on your assignment.

Maintaining relationships and staying connected with others doesn't mean losing sight of your purpose. It is about finding the right balance between personal growth and fostering relationships that can support and enhance your journey. By staying connected, you can receive support and inspiration as well as contribute to the growth and development of others. The goal is to maintain a healthy connection with others, creating a complementary balance in potentially each other's purpose assignments.

Communicate your purpose and vision. This fosters better alignment, draws support, and inspires others to participate in your mission. Your purpose assignment and story are powerful messages. Create a message that conveys the impact and importance of your purpose.

Below are considerations when you are intentional about building solid relationships.

- **Seek Guidance and Mentorship**: Engage with others who can serve as sounding boards and sources of encouragement. Find mentors, advisors, or individuals with experience in your field of purpose or who can align and support you with your goals.

- o Surround yourself with people who value your journey and respect your purpose assignment. Share your challenges and seek their insights. Their insights and guidance can provide valuable perspectives, help you avoid common pitfalls, and accelerate your progress as you focus on your purpose assignment.
- o Seek partnerships with groups and organizations that align with your purpose, leveraging their collective resources and expertise to amplify your impact.
- o Join communities related to your purpose and connect with like-minded individuals who can offer encouragement, support, and assistance.
- o Collaborate and partner with others who share a similar vision or complement your purpose. Collaborations can help expand your reach and provide you with additional resources.

- **Share your Message**: Share your purpose statement and connect with others on a deeper level. This can be done through written communication, presentations, social media, or conversations. Effective communication goes beyond just speaking and being heard. It involves validating others' perspectives, active participation in discussions, engagement with empathy, acceptance of differing viewpoints, and expressing gratitude for exchanging ideas. Developing strong communication skills helps foster positive relationships and promotes collaboration and understanding.

- o Create compelling stories that resonate with your audience and inspire them to support and engage with you.

o Practice conveying your message with clarity, enthusiasm, and authenticity.

- **Intentional Presence**: Staying present in your actions is important in executing your purpose. When engaging with others, be fully present and attentive. Always seek to engage and understand their perspectives, needs, and concerns.

    o Stay connected and open to hear from the Lord. Recognize that God is the source of your purpose and the One who empowers you to fulfill it. In all your endeavors, acknowledge His presence, seek His will, and give Him thanks. Cultivate a heart of gratitude and praise, acknowledging God's faithfulness and provision throughout your journey. Invite Him into every aspect of your life, and trust He is working out all things for your good.

    o Be open to hearing from trusted sources, including mentors, peers, and customers.

    o Listen intentionally to positive and constructive feedback to refine your approach and make necessary adjustments. Constructive criticism should be used as a tool for growth and improvement.

    o Learn from other's experiences and insights. This could play a role in your journey.

- **Be a PAAL** (Practice Active and Attentive Listening): Listening actively and attentively is a valuable skill that greatly enhances communication and understanding. This helps to discern your calling, the specific assignment, and the next steps. You will gain valuable insights into hearing the words spoken and paying attention to non-verbal cues, underlying emotions, and unspoken messages. The unspoken words, feelings, and nuances can often lead to understanding a situation's deeper needs, risks, or possibilities. This comprehensive listening approach allows you to fully engage in conversations, show empathy, and better understand the needs and perspectives of others. As you approach active listening with an open mind, compassion, and genuine curiosity, you create space for others to freely share their thoughts and perspectives. You can be present in the moment without rushing to judgment and interrupting them. By honing your active listening skills, you can uncover hidden information, understand others more deeply, and identify potential challenges or opportunities that may not be immediately apparent. As you engage in reflective conversations and ask thoughtful questions to foster a deeper understanding, you can connect more authentically and make more informed decisions.

Discerning what is meant for you and how to respond or act requires attentiveness and understanding. It involves interpreting the information received, aligning it with your values and goals, and making informed decisions. Discernment involves utilizing your intuition, experience, and insights from active listening to guide your actions. By honing your listening skills, practicing discernment, and cultivating effective communication:

o   You can navigate challenges more effectively.
o   Build stronger connections with others.
o   Respond thoughtfully to the situations that come your way.
o   Build a more straightforward path in your purpose journey.

Continue to work on building your active and attentive listening skills. Let them shape your journey toward fulfilling your purpose and making a positive impact.

o   **Acknowledge Your Emotions**: Effectively managing your interpersonal relationships will enhance your ability to navigate challenges and build meaningful connections. It's important to acknowledge and validate your feelings. Allow yourself to experience disappointment or frustration, but avoid getting consumed by them. Recognize that setbacks are a part of life's journey, and they don't define your worth or potential.

o **Develop self-awareness** to understand your strengths, weaknesses, and emotions.

o **Cultivate empathy** to relate to and understand the needs and perspectives of yourself and others.

o **View challenges as opportunities** for growth, innovation, and breakthroughs. Shift your perspective and explore alternative approaches or solutions. Sometimes, unexpected obstacles lead to discovering new paths and possibilities that can ultimately enhance your journey.

Part of acknowledging your worth is to deal with disappointment and rejection as they occur effectively. It is crucial to recognize the value of taking the time to acknowledge and genuinely feel your emotions. Understanding that rejection does not diminish your inherent worth is essential. Rather than viewing it as a setback, consider that rejection may redirect you away from an investment, partnership, or relationship incompatible with your goals and values. Express gratitude for the valuable insight gained through the experience. Embrace the rejection by acknowledging it as a stepping stone to growth and shift your focus toward the next steps in your journey. Remember, your worth remains intact, and each rejection is an opportunity to align with more fitting opportunities and experiences. As you embrace your challenges, be mindful of others in their journey and stay 'SHARP'.

- **The SHARP Approach**

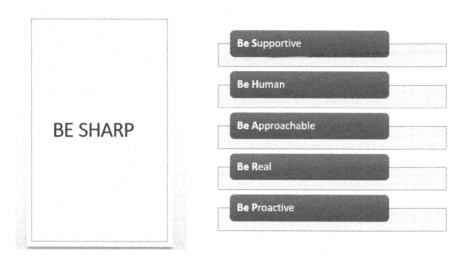

To navigate the intricacies of your purpose and effectively manage relationships, adopt a **SHARP** approach.

- o First and foremost, **support** others' callings, recognizing and encouraging their unique journeys.
- o Embrace **humanity**. Be authentic and vulnerable, and connect with others on a personal level.
- o **Approachability** is essential. Be someone others feel comfortable reaching out to, fostering an environment of open communication.
- o Be **real**. Authenticity builds trust and strengthens connections. Your genuine self is a powerful force in creating meaningful relationships.
- o Lastly, be **proactive**. Take initiative in nurturing connections, addressing challenges, and actively contributing to the growth of yourself and those around you.

A SHARP approach ensures a balanced and effective navigation of your purpose and the relationships accompanying your journey.

- **Conscious Connectivity**

The connectedness to oneself and others is an invaluable source of insight and clarity, a dynamic force that resonates throughout every area of life. This connection, formed through self-awareness and genuine understanding of others, is the key to unlocking a deeper understanding of the world and your place. You better understand the real you as you nurture a connectedness to yourself, embracing your thoughts, emotions, and aspirations. This self-awareness becomes a guiding light, clearing the path to your true purpose and allowing you to navigate life's complexities with a heightened sense of direction. Additionally, fostering a connection with others creates a unique synergy. Like-minded individuals are drawn to this shared spirit, creating a community that resonates with common values and goals. This collective consciousness becomes a powerful force, amplifying the impact of shared endeavors, which could lead to a common vision.

This connectedness plays a pivotal role in effective and impactful communication. The ability to authentically connect with others allows for a more meaningful exchange of ideas, fostering an environment where understanding, empathy, and collaboration flourish. Like a network of interconnected units, this shared consciousness and clarity form solid relationships, strengthening individual bonds and promoting a harmonious exchange of thoughts and perspectives.

Committing to being consciously connected within oneself and others is a transformative journey. It enhances personal growth, attracts those who resonate with you and your purpose, and lays the foundation for a conscious and solid union. Through this interconnectedness, communication becomes not just a transaction of words but a transparent exchange that breaks down barriers, fostering better understanding and contributing to the pursuit of real impact and effectiveness.

- **Life Savers vs Bystanders**

Distinguish between those who actively help in situations and those who merely observe. Surround yourself with individuals who are willing to prioritize your well-being without hesitation.

During a challenging drive on an extremely hot day in college, my exhaustion led to a major accident. Struggling to reach a rest stop, I crashed and totaled my car. I awakened to a crowd of concerned individuals who surrounded my vehicle on the highway. One lasting memory was the nurse, who I later learned was traveling in the opposite direction during the crash. Upon witnessing the accident, she immediately stopped her car. She bravely ran across the highway, and I faintly heard her calling to offer assistance without knowing the details or severity. At that moment, she chose to be a lifesaver instead of merely standing by to observe. She demonstrated genuine concern, was quick to act, and was willing to help in my time of need. You should seek and offer this level of support and commitment in your relationships.

Lifesavers naturally demonstrate:

- o **Genuine Support**: True life savers go beyond witnessing an event; they actively engage and assist. They have a genuine willingness to help.
- o **Empathy and Compassion**: Lifesavers often possess high empathy and compassion. They can put themselves in others' shoes, sensing when someone might be distressed and responding with care and urgency.

o **Selflessness**: Lifesavers prioritize the well-being of others over personal convenience or safety. They are selfless in their actions.

o **Reciprocal Relationships**: Building a network of lifesavers involves cultivating relationships based on mutual support and care. Being a lifesaver for others creates a reciprocal dynamic that strengthens connections.

o **Commitment to Well-being**: Lifesavers are committed to the well-being of those around them. They take action without hesitation, recognizing the importance of immediate assistance in critical situations.

Surround yourself with life savers who provide a healthy and supportive community. They will actively engage with you, stand with you in your challenges, and celebrate with you in your wins. These relationships foster a natural mindset of giving and receiving support, enriching the quality of your connections. Cultivating and appreciating such relationships can be essential for navigating life's challenges and joys.

 ## Manage Your Time Purposefully

In addition to cultivating meaningful relationships, continuously develop and improve the skills related to your purpose. Identify areas for growth and seek opportunities for learning and development. Identify the skills and knowledge relevant to your purpose and seek opportunities to enhance them. Eliminate distractions and create a productive environment that allows you the time to focus on your goals.

Focus on the things that truly matter, regardless of the assignment size. Your faith and willingness to act are more important than the scale of the task. Work on it in small increments of time, building upon each effort. When you feel tired and emotionally drained, turn to prayer and thanksgiving.

Similarly, continue praying and expressing gratitude when you experience success and achievements.

Invest in your personal and professional development related to your purpose and continuously seek opportunities to enhance your skills and broaden your expertise.

- **Research**: Conduct research through courses, workshops, books, and mentorship, gathering information about your purpose. Seek a better understanding of your assignment, target audience, specific needs, and trends. Ask questions for clarity and embrace your curiosity. This is the time for you to explore the possibilities of how to move forward. Review and update your purpose plan as you learn more.

- **Practice flexibility and adaptability**: Recognize that resources, skills, and the external environment may evolve and change. Be adaptable and willing to embrace new approaches and strategies as needed. Continuously evaluate and refine your resources and skills to stay relevant and practical.

- **Stay committed to learning and growth**: View challenges as opportunities for growth and development, continuously refining and expanding your resources, skills, and ability to articulate your vision. Instead of seeing setbacks as failures, view them as stepping stones to progress. Focus on improving, and continuously seek ways to develop your skills and mindset.

- **Self-care and balance**: Take care of yourself spiritually, physically, mentally, and emotionally throughout the process. Be kind to yourself during moments of frustration and disappointment. Practice self-compassion and understand that setbacks do not reflect your worth or ability. Give yourself the space and time to regroup, recharge, and refocus. Nurture a healthy work-life balance, practice self-reflection, and seek support when needed. Remember that your well-being is vital for sustained progress and fulfilling your purpose.

- **Be selfless in your work**: Focus on your work's impact on others. Value your effort rather than solely considering the time it took. The outcome of your actions will testify to your belief, obedience, and the process you have embraced.

 ## Give Back for a Greater Purpose

Effective and efficient giving becomes integral to that journey as you live in your purpose. It's not just a sporadic act of generosity but a consistent practice rooted in your mission to make a meaningful difference in the lives of others. The act of giving holistically involves a variety of methods. Faithful giving is heartfelt and is your powerful expression of generosity, compassion, and genuine desire to impact others positively. It includes tangible and intangible sacrifices.

Tangible forms of giving may include providing financial assistance, offering material possessions, or contributing your skills to a cause. It often addresses immediate and practical needs and demonstrates your willingness to alleviate the burdens of others. For example, post-surgery, I had several family members and friends reach out to offer a kind word and a helping hand. I distinctly remembered a message from my cousin who not only offered his prayers and thanksgiving for my recovery but unexpectedly offered financial assistance if I needed it. I was taken aback because I am not used to being on the receiving end, but his offer, knowing that I was not working, was very practical and spoke volumes. He understood I may have other needs beyond the best wishes and niceties. This was something tangible and useful that I may have needed.

On the other hand, intangible giving, equally important, involves your attention, empathy, and emotional support. This form of giving recognizes the importance of emotional connection and understanding of others. Praying, listening, offering a kind word, or providing a shoulder to lean on can profoundly impact someone's life. Post-surgery, my sister-in-law visited without being asked. Although her presence was tangible, her sitting with me and allowing me to be still without even speaking, and if you know us, that is not the norm, but the unspoken was intangible. It was much needed, appreciated, and priceless.

Combining material support and emotional connection creates a holistic approach to generosity. Giving is powerful for building connections, fostering empathy, and creating a sense of shared humanity. Giving should not be done because others can see it. It should demonstrate your genuine, heartfelt, and meaningful contribution. You gain the biggest reward when you can give without expecting anything. When giving is authentic, it becomes a powerful expression of selflessness. It drives a positive change, benefits typically the receiver, and brings the giver a sense of joy and fulfillment.

I find joy when someone reminds me of something that I did that I didn't even remember. Years could have passed by, but it still had an impact on them. It warms my heart because I know that whatever I did was meant to be. The other day, my sister mentioned that her church was reading *The Purpose Driven Life* by Rick Warren. She was excited because she didn't need to buy the book. She noted that I had gifted it to her. It must have been twenty years ago that I gave it to her. I read the book, and it was a blessing to me, and I wanted to share it with others. Her reminder was great timing, taking me back to why I wrote this book. I distinctly remember a comment in the book stating that we are all created for a purpose. I didn't know my purpose back then, but now, I am writing about what I have learned about purpose execution. This was a full-circle moment for me. The Lord provides us with revelations sometimes when they are most unexpected.

By fostering a mindset of giving without expectations, you contribute to building a more compassionate and supportive community and experiencing a profound sense of purpose and satisfaction that goes beyond external recognition. This approach to giving aligns with the idea that the most meaningful contributions are often those made with a pure and selfless heart.

Efficient giving is deliberate and strategic. It proactively offers the necessary resources to empower individuals to acquire knowledge and nurture their growth and development. As others pour into you, return the favor and pour it into people.

Giving back is necessary to live your life purpose,
as we are all expected to serve others.

Also, be honest about what you experienced on your purpose journey by sharing the wins and the struggles. Your honest view will assist others in executing their plans. By providing this insight, you offer more than just a personal narrative. It's a way of giving back to contribute to the growth and well-being of others on a similar journey.

Effective and Efficient giving should be:

Giving is a purpose-driven, strategic, and transformative approach to helping others. It recognizes the importance of equipping individuals with the proper support, skills, and resources to grow and thrive independently.

As you embrace your purpose, remember to extend assistance to others on their journey, empowering them to build and flourish.

Side note: Silent struggles

- The journey will likely get complex and overwhelming.

- Do not over-judge or beat yourself up.

- Celebrate that you have started and are on your way!

- Give others a chance to connect with you. Human connections are necessary and encouraged.

- Show up as your complete self. Be true to who you are.

- Reflect before reacting.

    o What do I need to know or learn in this challenge?
    o What do I need to do about it?

Sharing your struggles, challenges, and perseverance can profoundly impact others encountering similar obstacles. When you open up, it humanizes you by showing that, like everyone else, you face difficulties and challenges. This relatability can make others feel less alone in their struggles and more connected to you. You can empathize with others as you have had similar experiences. You are better able to bond and build trust with others. This can also inspire and motivate others as you overcome difficulties and achieve your goals.

In a culture that often emphasizes success and downplays difficulties, your openness about your struggles helps to normalize the idea that setbacks and challenges are a natural part of any journey. This can alleviate the shame or stigma that some people associate with adversity. People appreciate authenticity, and your willingness to share your story can create a sense of unity and support. By sharing, you offer more than just a personal narrative. You provide relatability, empathy, inspiration, problem-solving insights, encouragement, normalization of struggles, connection, and a path forward. It is a way of giving back and contributing to the growth and well-being of others who may have a similar journey.

Walk in **STRIDE.**

- Rely on your innate **strength** and ability.

- **Trust** the process.

- Be aware of your **reality**.

- Follow your **instincts**.

- Be **diligent** and progress forward.

- Stay **encouraged,** as this too shall pass.

Continue to stride confidently on your journey, drawing upon your innate strength and abilities. Ground yourself in the present moment's reality, embracing its challenges and opportunities. Trust your instincts as a guiding compass, allowing them to navigate you through the twists and turns of your path. Be diligent in your efforts, steadily progressing forward with purpose and determination. Even in the face of adversity, stay encouraged, knowing that challenges are transient and this too shall pass. Your perseverance and resilience are the pillars that will carry you through, transforming obstacles into stepping stones on your ongoing journey. Keep striding, relying on your internal fortitude and wisdom, and let each step be a testament to your unwavering commitment to personal growth and fulfillment.

Grooming and developing the necessary and relevant skills to support your purpose will increase your impact and bring your purpose to life. Remain dedicated to your growth and adapt as needed to navigate the ever-changing landscape of purposeful work. Remember that getting started is a crucial step toward realizing your purpose. Stay committed, persevere through challenges, and celebrate your progress. Each step forward brings you closer to fulfilling your purpose assignment.

Reflection – _Shadow View_

I finally listened and obediently resigned from my job. I have trusted the Lord, and now, walking, I am unapologetically in my calling. It took time to decide as I do not know the outcome. I've had several iterations of praying, thinking it through, and planning for it. And even with the forethought and plans, things did not go as I thought they would. It is not an easy process, but I am at peace and have found joy in the simple things—my health, my time, my family and friends, and just living each day with purpose.

The security of a regular paycheck provided comfort, but stepping into the unknown forced me to rely on His authority and provision. I am out of my comfort zone, dedicating most of my time to completing this book. This is my current priority. We often measure our worth by our financial state, title, possessions, or external validations, but I am reminded that I am of high value because of who I am in Christ. In acknowledging my identity in Him, I recognize the inherent worth bestowed upon me. This worth is not contingent on worldly standards but is grounded in the unchanging and boundless love and purpose He extends to me. I dedicate myself to this effort because I now recognize my inherent value.

There's a purposeful journey ahead, a destiny meant uniquely for me. The tasks are not random; they are precisely placed in my path. My work reflects my worth, and my ongoing investment in myself is beyond measure. It's a commitment to continuous growth, an acknowledgment that the value I bring to the world is priceless, and the effort I put in is an investment in my potential and purpose.

As I embrace my identity in Christ, I stand as a testament to each individual's profound value within the framework of their spiritual journey.

I am of good value and values. I am valued.

Proverbs 4: 7-8 (NIV)

[7] The beginning of wisdom is this: Get wisdom.
Though it costs all you have, get understanding.
[8] Cherish her, and she will exalt you;
embrace her, and she will honor you.

NOTES & INSIGHTS:

CHAPTER 4 FOCUS:
"Get in Motion"

Focus (Merriam-Webster definition): A center of activity, attraction, or attention.

FOCUS on your purpose-calling.

You are God's workmanship, created with a purpose. You are to focus on the work prepared for you to walk in. Concentrating on your purposes and assignments involves actively seeking out and embracing the specific tasks, roles, and responsibilities that have been ordained for you. It means recognizing that you were created uniquely and gifted to carry out your specific purpose. This requires a willingness to surrender your plans and desires to the Lord, allowing Him to direct your steps and reveal His purpose for your life. It goes beyond accomplishments and achievements. It involves living a life that is in harmony with the physical and spiritual, being intent on living out the fundamental values given to you above all else. You are expected to use your talents, abilities, and resources to serve others and bring glory to God.

Engaging in work that aligns with your values and brings meaning to your life can profoundly impact your overall well-being and sense of fulfillment.

As you cultivate an attitude of gratitude for your resources and blessings, your focus will shift from what you lack to what you have. You will better appreciate the freedom, purpose, and opportunities to pursue your true calling. You will be contented with living within your means and finding joy in the simple things. Discovering and fulfilling our purposes often requires a process of discernment and seeking God's wisdom. It requires you to:

- Step out of your comfort zone.

- Take known and unknown risks.

- Trust in God for guidance when the path seems uncertain or challenging.

Your most valuable pursuit is to focus on your life mission. You should invest your energy wholeheartedly into the task assigned to you. The rewards that will be produced from your effort will be beyond measure. Trust and believe you are entitled to receive what has been destined for you. Your steadfast commitment to pursuing your purpose is the force that will propel you forward. Recognizing that you cannot bring your goals and assignments to fruition without taking action is crucial. So, commit to actively engaging in the journey towards your purpose, for *it is through your actions that success is achieved*.

You will experience fulfillment and more profound satisfaction as you focus on your calling. Your life will become a testimony to His faithfulness and grace. You are a vessel through which His love and truth can be revealed to others.

Ephesians 2:10 (NIV) [10] *For we are his handiwork, created in Christ Jesus for good works, which God prepared in advance for us to do.*

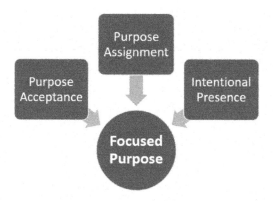

Accepting and focusing on your purpose are essential steps toward fulfilling it and progressing. It emphasizes the importance of understanding your purpose and dedicating your energy and attention to it. This becomes a crucial step in executing your purpose. It is recognizing that you have been chosen for a specific task or mission and are willing to embrace it wholeheartedly. This acceptance does not imply that you have all the answers or know exactly how to accomplish your purpose, but it signifies your readiness to embark on the journey and work through the details as they unfold. While pursuing your purpose, you will encounter individuals who will support you. Some may be intentionally assigned to assist you, while others may come into your life unexpectedly and offer valuable insights, assistance, and encouragement. Embracing the idea that you are not alone and that there are people who will contribute to your journey can provide comfort and empowerment. Remember to remain open to collaboration, be receptive to guidance, and appreciate the collective effort that can help you fulfill your purpose.

I lost focus over the years after I was entrusted with my purpose assignment. This book was an assignment given to me quite some time ago. I experienced various emotions, from being surprised, overwhelmed, nervous, excited, and even afraid. I did not know how to move forward and could not get out of my way. I started and stopped many times. I spoke about it with my inner circle, attended conferences, researched, and even supported others in their book-writing process and launches, but I could not move forward with my own. It was easy to keep busy without doing the actual work. The interesting thing is that the only work I needed to do was to be obedient. I am conscious of the potential missed opportunities for someone who may have needed this book sooner. I am giving myself grace and asking the Lord for forgiveness. I might miss the mark again, but I am moving forward in obedience and hope, putting focus on the assignment.

Do not confuse being busy as real progress.

If you are not intentional about staying focused and spending time on your tasks, your assignment will be stalled. It is understandable if you, too, have gone through moments of feeling stuck, questioning your readiness, and wrestling with feelings of unworthiness or lack of talent. These are common hurdles that many individuals face when embarking on their purpose assignment. You must recognize the state that you are in and take steps to overcome it.

Breaking through barriers that aim to keep you in a state of lack is essential. You know that your purpose was ordained and meant for you. In the moments of dryness, give praise and thanks for having the strength to acknowledge the season you are in. This will build up your endurance. It will also demonstrate your faith, providing opportunities for others to see how staying focused brings fruitful results. The perfect time to try something new and step outside your comfort zone by being courageous is when you await your breakthrough. Fear will keep you from benefitting from what is in store for you to receive. Remember that this transition period is temporary and part of the journey toward living a purposeful and fulfilling life. Stay committed to your calling, remain adaptable, and trust that tangible and intangible rewards will come soon.

Sometimes, believing in your calling and fully embracing your purpose assignment takes time and self-reflection. As stated, feeling overwhelmed or unsure about the journey is natural. Still, it is important not to let those feelings paralyze or prevent you from acting. Take the time to reflect on the triggers that make you uncomfortable or cause procrastination. Understand why these triggers have such an impact on you. Reflect on past experiences and patterns to gain insight into your reactions and behaviors. Giving yourself grace and seeking forgiveness is a part of the process. Though it is essential to acknowledge missed opportunities and delays, remember that everything happens in its perfect timing. Moving forward with your assignment, you can impact and reach those needing your specific project now.

To ensure you don't get in the way of progress and stay aligned with your purpose, it's important to address the internal obstacles and negative patterns that may hinder your forward movement. It is normal to have doubts or fear of missing the mark in the future, but with each step you take, you gain experience, grow in confidence, and learn valuable lessons. Remember to trust in the guidance and strength of the Lord as you continue on your journey. Embrace this opportunity with determination and a renewed sense of hope and purpose. Your commitment to focus and moving forward to completing your purpose assignment is commendable.

There is a causal relationship between your actions and the outcomes you desire. If you stay stuck and don't take action, you hinder the potential for positive change and growth in your life. By remaining in your comfort zone and clinging to familiar thoughts and behaviors, you limit your ability to explore new possibilities and experience the blessings and rewards of stepping into your purpose. The longer you remain stuck, the more delayed your ability to execute your purpose becomes. This is the causal situation with the purpose assignment. If you do X, then Y will happen. If you don't do X, then Y does not have a chance to occur. It may eventually get reassigned to someone else resulting in a missed blessing for you and those in your path.

The blessing, the lesson, the learning, and the reward
could be lost in the process if you remain stuck.

Get Unstuck

Motionless	Get in Motion	Consistent Motion
• **Question**: 'Why me?'	• **Question**: 'Could it really be?'	• **Question**: 'Why not me?'
• **Vision**: Closed, Limited	• **Vision**: Moderate insight	• **Vision**: Open, Seeking
• **Disposition**: Fear, Anger	• **Disposition**: Curious, Cautious	• **Disposition**: Inviting, Willing
• **Accountability**: None, 'Blame Game'	• **Accountability**: Limited, Sporadic	• **Accountability**: Aware, Ownership
• **Preparedness**: Not ready	• **Preparedness**: Reactive	• **Preparedness**: Proactive
• **Change**: Don't see a need	• **Change**: Recognizes need	• **Change**: Desire & willing to adapt
• **State**: STUCK	• **State**: SAFEGUARD	• **State**: SUSTAIN

Persistently being stuck may indicate that deeper, unresolved issues are lingering beneath the surface and have been masked. It is necessary to unwrap the nicely packaged exterior to expose and address the core elements keeping you in a rut. We inadvertently train ourselves to retain pain and adversity within, leading to perpetual stagnation and lack of progress.

Proper forward motion is hindered when
emotional matters are left unattended.

Unlocking the intricacies of what is held within involves acknowledging and processing emotions that may have been suppressed. Whether rooted in hurt or hardship, these emotions are barriers to personal growth and can impede the journey toward a more fulfilling life. Dealing with these emotions is vital in breaking free to get in motion. Real motion is contingent on confronting and navigating through the complexities of your emotional landscape. By unraveling the layers and addressing the core issues, you pave the way for genuine progress, personal development, and a more authentic sense of well-being. Getting in proper motion requires emotional self-awareness and active engagement with your inner struggles for a meaningful and transformative journey.

Now and then, I check the weight of my emotional bucket. I focus on releasing the things that continue to weigh me down. This creates space for better clarity, more balance, and continued growth. Practicing this mindful approach allows you to prioritize your mental well-being and make room for a healthier and more balanced life. Being self-aware allows you to lessen your emotional burden and better enables you to discover what is essential for your evolution. Getting unstuck requires a conscious effort to break free from old patterns, challenge your comfort zones, and take action. Doing so creates the space for new opportunities, lessons, and rewards to unfold as you align with your purpose.

I tend to get disappointed by the lack of timeliness of others' follow-ups and responses when I am in my focused zone. I make up scenarios in my head as to what is causing the delays, which can quickly get me in the stuck zone. I have been better at being more open with letting others in the process, expecting it to get me out or keep me from the stuck zone. I apply this approach when I know I am sabotaging my assignment and creating barriers to what God has purposed me with. It has taken me many years to complete this book as I was stuck due to not having written anything before. I am not a writer. I am unqualified to write a book, I thought. In conversation with my coach in one of my stuck moments, I was introduced to a group that happily included me in their weekly writing meetings. At the end of the first meeting, the host stated, "Congratulations, you are now a writer!" They ended with that every meeting. It started as one hour of writing twice per week. I wasn't judged, no questions asked, just sharing space and time with others committed to writing. That was a big step in getting unstuck as I was excited to join them as much as possible to focus on my purpose assignment. I had no idea how seasoned most of these individuals were. They are professionals in their field and have many published works. That never came up in the introductions or on the calls. The group's only intent to write for that assigned time. How awesome is that? I am in motion and have since been consistently working to complete this purpose-driven assignment.

To move beyond the stuck zone to the sustain zone, it's essential to culti-vate a mindset of openness, adaptability, and courage. This may likely require assistance from others. Trust your village and lean into them for support during this time. Try not to keep your frustrations or internalize what you may deem as failure bottled up. Release the tension by giving yourself grace and focus on what's ahead. Staying the course and maintaining focus are essential when facing challenges or obstacles. Acknowledging difficulties may arise even with exceptional skills or abilities, is important. However, by staying committed and determined, you can navigate through them.

I sometimes reflect on the memory of a determined little girl with a burning desire to go on a school trip. However, she did not want to tap into her mother's resources as her mom was already working three jobs to care for her older siblings abroad. Undeterred by the lack of available funds, she embarked on a resourceful journey through her neighborhood. Armed with determination, she started collecting empty bottles, each worth five cents when returned. She steadily focused on her goal and gladly moved forward with her plan. Her grit and fearlessness shone brightly as she embraced unconventional means to achieve her dream. Undaunted by others' perceptions or potential judgment, she continued her mission. She even invited her friends who wanted to hang out. Her efforts bore fruit, and as the collection of bottles grew, so did her sense of accomplishment. Eventually, she earned the twenty dollars needed for the school trip.

As time passed, the memory of this innocent girl served as an inspiration for me when faced with blocked paths and limited resources. I admire my determination, strength, and the fearless pursuit of my dreams back then. As I get older, I yearn for that same level of fearlessness. It takes more energy now, but I think it is mainly due to an apprehension of judgment. I cherish the memory of this brave little girl and use her as a reminder that, even in challenging times, a keen focus on the goal, coupled with an unapologetic determination, can pave the way forward.

Maintain Focus

Sometimes, our self-doubt and insecurities can hold us back from taking action and embracing our true calling. No matter how prepared and focused you are, there will be times when all seems to be going against the plan. Everything that you thought would happen is not coming to fruition. It becomes frustrating for you to think or process what can be done next. Frustration can get the better part of you. You are human. Give yourself empathy and grace. This assignment is meant for you. What you are going through is a part of the process. I get my most significant breakthroughs when facing challenges that appear to be breaking me. Instead, there is hope that allows me to make it through whatever circumstances I may have to improve and go beyond what I could have imagined.

Challenges and setbacks are a natural part of any journey, including pursuing your purpose.

- *Setbacks and challenges do not define your purpose or its significance.*

- *They are stepping stones that shape and refine you along the way.*

You will inevitably encounter difficulties and face challenging situations. How you process and handle these challenges can significantly impact your journey. It is natural to feel fear or uncertainty. However, rather than succumbing to fear, you can choose to use faith as a powerful tool to combat and tackle the known and unknown challenges that lie ahead. Challenges and setbacks are not permanent. They are part of your journey. You are equipped to pass through it, strengthened by the experiences and lessons learned. Remain vigilant by keeping your mind focused and your heart steadfast. Stay out of your head. Avoid overthinking and excessive self-doubt. Instead, focus on taking action and moving forward. When negative thoughts arise, acknowledge them, but don't dwell on them. Reframe them into positive affirmations and remind yourself of your capabilities. Embrace the process and learn from the difficulties, keeping your focus on the bigger picture. Stay resilient, trust in your journey, and continue to pursue your purpose with passion and determination.

Maintain your focus and stay rooted and grounded in your purpose to foster growth and opportunities. There will be seasons of stillness, as your progress is not always linear. There will be times when opportunities appear to be lacking and non-existent. This is your dry season. Build yourself up by praying and giving praise. You will need to seek out being grateful for the smallest of things. Avoid portraying yourself as lacking. It is a mindset. Make it known that you are believing and expecting your breakthrough. Prepare for your blessings. I encourage and support you in staying focused and connected to your purpose. Continually remind yourself of the purpose behind your assignment. Reflect regularly on your calling and its impact. Find ways to measure progress beyond surface rewards, such as tracking personal growth, constructive feedback from others, and accomplishments. This will help you stay motivated and committed.

Consistent Motion

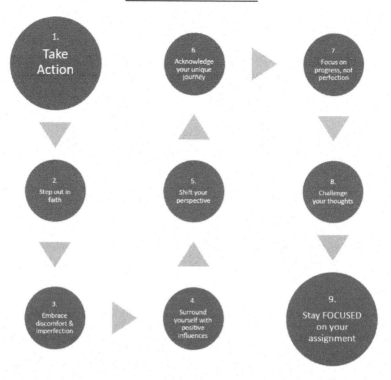

1. **Take action**: Break the cycle of stagnation by taking intentional steps forward. Start with small actions that align with your purpose and build momentum over time. Remember that consistent effort leads to significant results, even if progress feels slow.

2. **Step out in faith**: Be willing to take calculated risks outside your comfort zone. Growth and progress often come from embracing new challenges and opportunities that push you beyond your limits.

3. **Embrace discomfort and imperfection**: Recognize that growth and progress often come from being stretched and going beyond the unknown and unfamiliar. Challenge yourself to try new things, take calculated risks, and embrace the discomfort that comes with unfamiliar territory. Don't wait for perfection before taking action. Understand that mistakes and setbacks are part of the learning

process. Embrace imperfection and be willing to adjust your course along the way.

4. **Surround yourself with positive influences**: Continue to engage with supportive communities, mentors, or accountability partners who can encourage and inspire you on your journey. These connections can provide valuable insights, guidance, and encouragement to help you navigate through challenges. Surround yourself with a supportive network of mentors, peers, or friends who can provide guidance, encouragement, and accountability. Share your goals and progress with them, and lean on their support when you face challenges.

5. **Shift your perspective**: It is okay to lack knowledge but be open to learning and growth. View every opportunity, challenge, or setback as a chance to develop new skills, gain experience, and expand your knowledge.

6. **Acknowledge your unique journey**: Remember that everyone starts somewhere, and experience or titles don't define your worth or ability to pursue your purpose. Your journey is unique to you, and the important thing is that you're taking steps to move forward and grow.

7. **Focus on progress, not perfection**: Instead of striving for perfection or comparing yourself to others, celebrate your progress and the small victories along the way. Recognize that every step you take, no matter how small, brings you closer to fulfilling your purpose. Adopt a mindset that sees setbacks and failures as opportunities for learning and growth. Embrace the idea that you can develop new skills, acquire knowledge, and overcome obstacles through perseverance and a willingness to learn from experiences.

8. **Challenge your thoughts**: Become aware of self-limiting beliefs or negative thought patterns that keep you stuck. Challenge these

thoughts by replacing them with positive affirmations, focusing on your strengths, and seeking evidence of past accomplishments and successes.

9. **Stay FOCUSED on your assignment**: Stay focused on the assignment and purpose you've been called to. Remind yourself of its impact and value, regardless of external factors or limitations. Trust that as you stay committed and take consistent action, doors, and opportunities will open.

Setting the pace and remaining in constant motion is essential. As you wait on the Lord and seek His guidance, be open to hearing from Him and working in alignment with His will. Embrace the task you were given, knowing it was meant for you. Do not fear being chosen or taking a non-conventional path. Rise above the noise and tap into all the resources available to you. You can navigate your journey and fulfill your purpose with hope, faith, and a grateful heart. Trust in God's plan and yourself as you continue to move forward. The journey may have its ups and downs, and there may be moments of doubt and setbacks. But as long as you stay connected to your purpose, remain resilient, and keep taking those small steps forward, you will continue to make progress and fulfill the assignment you've been given. Keep believing in yourself and the work you are called to do.

Allowing yourself the space for a good cry when disappointment strikes is an act of self-compassion. Releasing the frustration becomes crucial in making room for inner peace and comfort. It's essential to love yourself enough to acknowledge and empathize with the emotions accompanying setbacks. The toll that roadblocks take on your physical and emotional well-being should not be underestimated. Therefore, creating a dedicated space to process these feelings is important. While withdrawing temporarily is natural, resist the urge to shut others out entirely. Instead, take moments of stillness without isolating yourself. Use your voice, whether it's through prayer or reaching out to supportive friends and family. Recognize that experiencing disappointment is integral to your growth, and you are not alone amidst the loneliness. Seek solace in the understanding of your supporters, who can listen and offer comfort, helping you navigate through the challenges and emerge stronger on the other side.

Practice Self Care

A part of keeping and maintaining focus is to practice self-care. Proper self-care and focus will assist with keeping up the momentum and finding renewed inspiration if you are in a rut or feel stuck. Ensure you care for your spiritual, physical, mental, and emotional well-being. Your overall care is essential for sustaining your efforts and maintaining clarity of purpose. Prioritize self-care activities in your routine that help you recharge. Ensure you maintain a healthy work-life balance and establish boundaries to prevent burnout. This can include fellowship, worship, exercise, spending time in nature, proper nutrition, sufficient rest, stress management, de-cluttering, or engaging in hobbies that bring you joy. Caring for yourself gives you the energy and resilience to stay committed to your purpose.

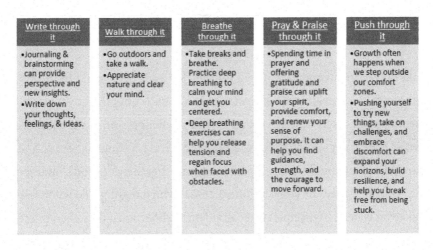

Write through it	Walk through it	Breathe through it	Pray & Praise through it	Push through it
•Journaling & brainstorming can provide perspective and new insights. •Write down your thoughts, feelings, & ideas.	•Go outdoors and take a walk. •Appreciate nature and clear your mind.	•Take breaks and breathe. Practice deep breathing to calm your mind and get you centered. •Deep breathing exercises can help you release tension and regain focus when faced with obstacles.	•Spending time in prayer and offering gratitude and praise can uplift your spirit, provide comfort, and renew your sense of purpose. It can help you find guidance, strength, and the courage to move forward.	•Growth often happens when we step outside our comfort zones. •Pushing yourself to try new things, take on challenges, and embrace discomfort can expand your horizons, build resilience, and help you break free from being stuck.

Refer to the Self-Care Schedule to create your routine - Template 7 in the Appendix: Item # Activity → Action Taken → Frequency.

Self-Care Schedule Example

Item #	Activity	Action Taken	Frequency
1	Prayer	I pray and reflect on the thoughts/people at the top of my mind, remembering to give thanks for all things.	*Daily – multiple times throughout the day.*
2	Self-Reflection	Inner thoughts when intentionally taking a walk or finding quiet time to be still.	*Casually throughout the day.*
3	Self-Acknowledgement / Acceptance	I am statements… I am blessed; I am bold; I am a giver; I am thankful.	*Aim for daily. Tap in when I feel stressed or challenged.*
4	Phone a friend	Call a friend or someone on my crew just because. During drives, walking or sometimes when I feel I have had too much screen time (i.e., binge-watching a show).	*At least 1 – 2 times weekly.*

Prayer

Make prayer an integral part of your journey. Set aside dedicated time to commune with God, seeking His guidance, wisdom, and strength. Pray for clarity, direction, and discernment as you navigate challenges and make decisions. Involve others in your journey by joining prayerful meetings, where you can share your challenges, seek support, and pray together for God's intervention. I recently read the story in John 6:16-21, which highlighted when Jesus walked on water. His disciples were afraid on the boat when they encountered the storm and rough waters. They were even more fearful when they saw a figure walking on the water towards the boat. Although it was a terrifying situation, I can only imagine their fear could have been lessened had they prayed. Prayer keeps us in connection with the Lord. Had they prayed during the storm, would they have been more in-tuned and recognized that Jesus was walking towards them? Why did they not initially call out to the Lord or lift their voices in prayer? God is with us in all storms.

By praying and acknowledging God's presence and guidance in all things, you create an environment that fosters spiritual growth, deepens your connection with God, and strengthens your ability to execute your purpose with faith and confidence. You are not alone in this journey, and the Lord is always ready to walk with you every step of the way.

Additional considerations:

When done with guidance and proper consideration for your health, *fasting* can be a spiritual practice that enhances focus, discipline, and clarity. It can be a way to break free from distractions and deepen your connection with your purpose. Be conscious of the quality and quantity of what you are eating. Hydrate, hydrate, hydrate.

Taking breaks and self-reflection are essential components of the journey. Take the time to nurture and prioritize your well-being. Taking care of yourself allows you to preserve your energy and love, appreciate your gifts, and enjoy the journey. Quick breaks are a great way to regain focus and reenergize yourself.

Celebrate your progress, acknowledge your efforts, and permit yourself to recharge. Take a moment to give yourself the praise you deserve for your incredible journey and accomplishments. Reflect on the challenges you've overcome, the growth you've experienced, and the milestones you've achieved. Acknowledge your hard work, perseverance, and dedication. Celebrate both the small victories and the significant milestones. Recognizing and praising yourself is an essential act of self-compassion and motivation. You are the author of your story, and every step forward is a testament to your strength and resilience. So, honor your journey and embrace the accomplishments that have shaped the remarkable person you are today.

By incorporating these methods into your life, you can overcome obstacles and stagnation, gain fresh insights, and build up your strength and focus as you continue moving forward with purpose and clarity.

Positioned

You will perform at your highest potential when you are positioned and purpose-filled. Achieving your highest potential is not merely about skill or effort but finding that sweet spot where strategic positioning converges with purposeful living. Your superpower, that unique quality within you, comes to life when you are in the correct position and aligned with your overarching purpose. The synergy created by the awareness of your assignment and your deep sense of purpose fulfillment creates the ideal conditions for optimal performance. As you navigate toward your goals, being both strategically positioned and intensely focused will propel you toward success. In this state, there's a natural flow and harmony in your circumstances, guided by an unwavering commitment to your life's project. It is at this point that the extraordinary becomes achievable. Aligning with your purpose and divine plan for fulfillment will empower you to perform effectively. Stay focused and remind yourself of your assignment. You are meant to do this project. Even though I had clarity on my purpose, I could not effectively execute the plan until I was in the right mindset, giving myself the space and freedom to be present and see the possibilities of what could be if I stayed on task. It is a balancing act of finding the right pace, staying focused, and determined.

Your purpose is your miracle waiting to be manifested. Be open to stepping out of your comfort zone and trust the process.

<u>Reflection</u> - *Bed of Clouds View*

Do not compare your calling to someone else's success, failure, or inability to see your talent or gift. You may not be the best person for this assignment, but you have been assigned to do your best. This book was delayed because I did not see myself as a writer. But do I need to be a writer to write? When my purpose was given to me, it didn't state any qualifications other than obeying the assignment. So again, why did it take me so long to complete this work?

Galatians 6:9 (NIV) - [9] ***Let us not become weary of doing good, for at the proper time we will reap a harvest if we do not give up.***

There will be doubt, defeat, and confusion along the way. During those times, remember that setbacks and difficulties are part of refining. Delays are expected and don't necessarily equate to failure. Sometimes, projects take longer than expected due to unforeseen circumstances, challenges, or personal growth and development. It's essential to view delays as learning and refinement opportunities rather than failure indicators. Stay focused on the assignment, trust in God's faithfulness, and persevere through the challenges with determination. May you reflect, relate, and release to be your best self, daily.

Remember, the journey is just as important as the destination. As you faithfully carry out your assignment, you will be transformed into the person God intends you to be. Embrace the growth from the journey, knowing that the process shapes and prepares you for greater things. Trust the process, learn from it, and continue to persevere.

Thank you Lord, for today. Thank you for waking me up and allowing me to take another breath. Thank you Lord, for all the little things you do that I do not think about, but over which You, God, have control. I am thankful for the insights and reminders of your presence and greatness. Thank you for thinking of me and gifting me with a purpose.

Proverbs 4: 5-6 (NIV)

[5] Get wisdom, get understanding;
do not forget my words or turn away from them.

[6] Do not forsake wisdom, and she will protect you;

love her, and she will watch over you.

NOTES & INSIGHTS:

CHAPTER 5 EXECUTE:
"Follow Through"

Execute (Merriam-Webster definition): *To carry out or put completely into effect.*

It is not enough to have a sense of purpose; you must actively pursue it and engage in the required meaningful work. Fulfilling your purpose requires the power of personal action. By being obedient, you will witness firsthand how stepping out in faith and taking decisive steps can lead to transformative outcomes.

Effective execution requires your faith and your action. Your active and deliberate participation is required to fulfill your purpose.

You will encounter and need to address common challenges and obstacles that arise during the execution phase by utilizing the outlined strategies to overcome them. From managing time and resources effectively to staying motivated and resilient, you will gain valuable insights into navigating the complexities of executing your purpose. Purpose execution involves several key elements and considerations to ensure you stay on track and make progress toward your goals.

3rd Phase: Purpose Execution

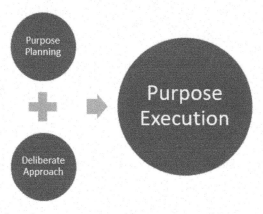

Key points to consider when executing your purpose:

- **Be consistent**: Take consistent and intentional action toward your plan. Maintain momentum by following through on the tasks that you have identified, taking the necessary steps to start the execution of your plan, and implementing them one by one. Remember that progress is often made through consistent action and learning from successes and failures. Break through any fear or hesitation and start implementing your plan. Progress is more important than perfection, so don't be afraid to learn and iterate. In writing this book, I utilized my idle time to write once I maintained focus. I also scheduled time on my calendar as a regular activity.

- **Get organized**: Track your progress, deadlines, and key information related to your assignment. Utilize tools such as the purpose plan you created. Follow up with to-do lists and calendars to stay organized, ensuring nothing falls through the cracks.

- **Stay the course**: Stay committed to your purpose and persevere through the obstacles and setbacks. Develop resilience and learn from failures along the way. Build resilience by developing a mindset that embraces challenges and setbacks as opportunities for growth. Cultivate a positive outlook and keep pushing forward, even when things get tough. Launching your purpose requires time, effort, and patience. Trust in your purpose and your ability to make a meaningful difference.

- **Focus on priorities**: Avoid distractions and stay focused on your priorities. Be mindful of time-wasting activities or projects that may divert your attention from your purpose. Learn to say no to commitments that don't align with your goals.

- **Celebrate small wins and milestones**: Acknowledge and celebrate the milestones and achievements. Recognize the progress and celebrate your accomplishments, no matter how small, and use it as motivation to keep moving forward. Acknowledging your progress and giving yourself credit for your steps will boost your motivation and reinforce your commitment. I would share with my husband and others in my support network when I had a breakthrough or learned something new. It kept me going and helped me hold myself accountable for the task.

- **Embrace risk and failure**: Launching your purpose often involves taking risks and facing the possibility of failure. Embrace these challenges as opportunities for growth and learning, make the necessary adjustments, and keep moving forward. Adaptability and flexibility are key in navigating the ever-evolving journey of purpose. As circumstances change or new opportunities arise, be willing to adjust your approach while staying true to the core of your purpose. Throughout the process, I have submitted excerpts of the book in competitions. The focus was not on winning; it allowed me to continue writing and learning along the way.

- **Reflect, learn, and share**: Take time to reflect on your progress, lessons learned, and areas for improvement. Continuously assess and adjust your strategies and actions based on feedback and new insights. Embrace a mindset that values learning and continuous improvement. Recognizing your progress will boost your motivation and reinforce your commitment to the task. Please share your insights and stories with others, inspiring and empowering them on their purposeful journeys.

- **Seek feedback and iterate**: Throughout the launch process, seek feedback from trusted resources who will provide constructive insights. This continuous process allows you to refine your plan as needed. Stay open to feedback and be willing to make the necessary changes to improve your impact.

- **Be mindful and patient**: Practice mindfulness to stay present and aware of your thoughts and emotions. Notice when negative patterns arise, and consciously choose not to let them derail you. Patience is key, as progress takes time. Trust the process and stay committed to your purpose.

- **Pray and be proactive**: Use it to seek guidance, clarity, and strength. Combine this with proactive action to address your challenges. Take small steps towards your goals, even if they feel uncomfortable or uncertain. Action is essential in moving forward.

- **Clarify your why**: Continuously remind yourself of your purpose's underlying reasons and motivations. Understanding why your purpose matters to you will help you stay committed and focused, especially during challenging times.

- **Stay connected with your purpose**: Regularly revisit and reaffirm your intention by visualizing the outcomes you seek to achieve. Review and repeat your purpose statement to keep it alive in your mind and heart.

Executing your purpose is a dynamic and ongoing process. Be adaptable, open to learning, and willing to adjust as you progress. Stay focused by maintaining a positive attitude and embrace the journey as you make meaningful progress toward accomplishing your purpose. By embracing the calling you received, continue to seek God's guidance, listen to His voice, and align your life with His will. It requires surrender, obedience, and faithfulness to His leading. Executing your purpose also requires a commitment to growth and transformation. It means allowing the Holy Spirit to work in you, shaping your character, and equipping you with the necessary gifts, talents, and abilities to fulfill your calling. It involves continuous learning, seeking wisdom, and developing the skills needed to carry out the tasks assigned to you effectively.

Remember that the journey itself is significant. It's not just about reaching a destination or accomplishing specific goals but about growth, development, and intimate fellowship with God. You are called to embrace and enjoy the journey, trusting that God is with you every step of the way. As you encounter challenges, obstacles, and moments of uncertainty, draw on your strength from knowing you are not alone. As your Sponsor, God has promised to be with you, to provide for you, and to empower you for the tasks He has assigned. You rely on His grace, wisdom, and strength to navigate your difficulties.

Purpose execution also involves a heart of service and love for others. You are meant to use your gifts and abilities to bless and uplift those around you, seeking to impact their lives positively. It requires a genuine concern for the well-being and interests of others as you strive to reflect the love and compassion of Christ. You are not just a passive recipient of your assignment but an active player who is called to execute and carry out the plan for your life. Just as a project requires diligent attention and review to ensure its success, your life assignments require ongoing care and oversight. You will continually monitor and update the plan as needed.

You will be referencing the plan that you created. Refer to Chapter 3. See the example below. Adjustments have been made to account for the timeframe and addition of new tasks.

Purpose Plan Example (updated) – Template 4

Activity / Task (Start with an action)	Resource	Actual Timeframe (Start / End Date)	Duration (i.e. Days, Weeks, Months)	Status (Not started, In Progress, Complete)
Write the book	Self	*2013 - 2023*	1 - 3 Years	*In Progress*
Identify the title	Self	*2013*	2 Weeks	*Complete*
Fine-tune the title	Self	*2013*	1 Month	*Complete*
Research how to be a writer	Self, friends with published books, online research	*Ongoing*	Daily	*Complete*
Pray & and ask for guidance	Self, bible study group	*Ongoing*	Daily	*In Progress*
Prepare content outline	Self, Advisor	*2013 - 2023*	2 Months	*Complete*
Milestone: 1ˢᵗ draft of book title and content outline completed	Self	*2013 - 2014*	1 Month	*Complete*
Determine Audience	Self, Sponsor (God)	*2013 - 2023*	Ongoing	*Complete*
Research the Book creation process	Self, Online, Conferences, Other Writers	*2013 - 2023*	Ongoing	*Complete*
Seek out / Join Groups/support system	Self, Writing groups/clubs/organizations	*2019 - 2023*	Ongoing	*Complete*
Milestone: Gained more insights on writing a book and joined a support group	Self	*2022*		*Complete*
Write each chapter	Self	*2015 - 2023*	Ongoing	*Complete*
Milestone: Chapter X is completed	Self	*2015 - 2023*		*Complete*
Review and edit the chapters	Self, Editor(s)	*2023 - 2024*	Ongoing	*In Progress*
Publish the book	Self	*2024*	Ongoing	*In Progress*
Final Milestone: The book is written and complete	Self, Sponsor	*2024*		*In Progress*

You will review and gauge the progress and take corrective action when necessary to keep your assignment on track. Monitoring your tasks will keep you focused and aligned to nurture and sustain your purpose. It is important to stay attentive and engaged in your purpose project. Accountability is essential for monitoring your progress and ensuring intentional action.

Recognizing that you are not meant to navigate your assignments alone, you will discover the value of seeking support from mentors, accountability partners, and the community.

As you progress through the execution phase, you will understand the cyclical nature of your purpose and the importance of continuous evaluation and improvement. You are encouraged to celebrate milestones and achievements while remaining vigilant in identifying areas requiring attention and refinement. In assessing progress, identify areas for improvement and make the necessary adjustments. Purpose execution requires actionable steps to ensure that you maintain alignment with the purpose plan for your life.

By embracing the practices of monitoring and follow-through, you will cultivate resilience, adaptability, and a deep sense of purpose. Your assignments will be nurtured and sustained, allowing you to make a lasting impact by the ordained plan for your life. You have been empowered with the knowledge, tools, and motivation to monitor and follow through on your purpose effectively.

Purpose execution is not about achieving perfection or completing everything. It is staying obedient to the tasks and assignments that are meant for you. By consistently taking action, addressing impediments, and embracing the journey, you bring your purpose to life and make a unique impact. Staying the course on executing your purpose is a journey requiring perseverance, dedication, and a deep belief in the value and impact of your purpose. Stay aligned with your vision, keep learning and growing, and trust your ability to make a meaningful difference.

Reflection - _Aerial view_

The Lord plans to utilize us in many ways. His perfect and divine plan is individually made and is given to you as your purpose. My purpose in writing this book was made clear time and time again. Executing this purpose assignment required active pursuit and engagement. Although I knew about the project, I had to actively participate and move forward with it. Your purpose requires nurturing and cultivating. It will take dedication, effort, and commitment to bring your purpose to fruition.

This book is just one manifestation of the many assignments and projects assigned to me. Each endeavor uniquely expresses my purpose; through them, I can make an impact and fulfill my divine assignment. As you continue executing your divine purpose, may you find strength, guidance, and fulfillment in knowing that you are an instrument of God's plan and that each step you take brings you closer to completion. You are loved, admired, and appreciated just as you are. Stay committed to your path and enjoy the journey along the way. Embrace that you are unique and have special qualities and strengths.

Avoid the temptation to overcompensate for any perceived shortcomings. Instead, focus on educating, enlightening, and entertaining others with your knowledge and talents. Take action on your plans and put them into motion, knowing you have what it takes to make a positive impact. Don't be afraid to color outside the lines, creating your borders while redefining the standards.

Believe in yourself and trust in your abilities.

You are enough, and your unique perspective and contributions are valuable.

Keep shining your light and making a difference in the lives of others.

Proverbs 4:1-2 (NIV)

[1] Listen, my sons, to a father's instruction;
pay attention and gain understanding.
[2] I give you sound learning,
so do not forsake my teaching.

NOTES & INSIGHTS:

CHAPTER 6 LEARNINGS:
"Review and Reflect"

Learning (Merriam-Webster definition): Knowledge or skill acquired by instruction or study.

Just BEcause

I desire to BE me at all times

Not how I am expected to BEhave or what they want me to BEcome.

I am a BEacon of light

and

Leave BEauty everywhere I go

I am living my BEst life

I BElieve in me

BEcause He created me to

BE.

Lisa P-S

Reflecting on your purpose and sharing lessons learned is essential for personal growth and development in your life journey. Take time to look back on the experiences related to the challenges, successes, and failures you encountered while pursuing your purpose. Consider how these experiences have shaped you and what you have learned about yourself. This can provide insight into your next assignment and your continued fulfillment of your life's purpose. You have gained skills and knowledge that are contributing to your growth. Ensure you shift your focus from blame to reflection. Please do not get stuck by lingering or dwelling on what went wrong; instead, focus on what can be done. Ask yourself what lessons can be learned from the situation. Look for areas where you can take responsibility and make improvements. This shift in mindset empowers you to grow and find solutions.

Reflections on your purpose are personal and unique to your journey. Share your insights with honesty, vulnerability, and a genuine desire to help yourself and others. By doing so, you continue to grow in your life journey and can inspire and motivate others to continue to pursue their purpose. Highlight the tools, strategies, or support systems that helped you navigate difficult times. Provide insights into how you bounced back from setbacks and failures and the lessons you learned about resilience and determination. These insights can inspire others to overcome their challenges. Embrace your mistakes as valuable learning opportunities and share the lessons you gained from them. Transparency about your own mistakes can provide guidance and encouragement to others. Share how you have embraced the willingness to learn from new experiences.

Please encourage others to be open to learning and adapting their approach as they pursue their purpose. Reflect on the moments of gratitude and celebration throughout your purpose journey. Acknowledge the milestones, accomplishments, and support you received along the way. Express gratitude for the opportunities and lessons that have come your way. Use your reflections and lessons learned to encourage and inspire others on a similar path. Share your authentic experiences and insights to motivate and empower others to pursue their purpose passionately.

Questions and Considerations

1. What are the key insights and lessons you have gained from living your purpose?

2. What have you discovered about your strengths, weaknesses, values, and passions?

3. What is the impact your purpose has had on others?

4. How have you made a difference in their lives?

5. What feedback or testimonials have you received that validate the value of your purpose?

6. What are the challenges and obstacles you faced along the way?

7. What were the most significant hurdles, and how did you overcome them?

8. How has pursuing your purpose transformed you as a person?

9. What personal growth, character development, and mindset shifts have you experienced?

10. How have you evolved, and how has this transformation impacted your overall well-being?

11. Have you encountered moments when you had to demonstrate resilience and perseverance?

12. How did you handle your mistakes or missteps during your purpose journey?

13. What is the importance of continuous learning and adaptation in pursuing your purpose?

Have you ever fallen and hurt yourself while doing an activity? Naturally, you will be more cautious the next time you perform that action. It served as a reminder if you were also left with a scar. Your approach to challenges and how you solve them will shape your healing and growth.

Your choices in handling difficulties influence the outcome, lessons learned, and emotional or spiritual scars that may linger.

This is crucial as it impacts your overall well-being and development.

<u>Reminders</u>

Real-life lessons can be learned when we face obstacles and challenges that are overwhelming and out of our control. To get out of the rut, re-energize, refocus, and roll out your purpose-driven plan. Take time to reflect on your situation and the cause. The challenges that you face provide opportunities for further learning and development. Consider the aspects of your plan or approach that might need adjustment or improvement. Review past successes and learnings to gain insights for moving forward.

Conduct a recap or evaluation of your progress and the effectiveness of your actions.

- Identify what has been working well and what hasn't.
- Explore any patterns or obstacles that have contributed to you feeling stuck.

Assess your plan and identify areas that need refinement or restructuring.

- If necessary, break down your goals into smaller, manageable tasks or milestones.
- Consider if any adjustments or changes are needed to align better with your purpose and desired outcomes.

Remind yourself of your divine purpose and the significance of your work.

- Spend time in prayer or meditation, seeking guidance and renewed clarity.
- Revisit your initial motivations and the impact you hope to make.
- Embrace your frustrations as a learning opportunity. Assess your approach, identify areas for improvement, and adapt your strategies.
- Hold onto the belief that things can and will improve. Setbacks are temporary.

Take care of your physical, emotional, and spiritual well-being.

- Engage in activities that rejuvenate and inspire you, such as exercise, hobbies, spending time in nature, or connecting with loved ones.
- Seek out sources of motivation and inspiration, such as reading books, listening to podcasts, or attending conferences or events related to your purpose.

- Reach out to your accountability partners, mentors, or trusted individuals who can provide sound guidance, encouragement, and perspective.

Identify your priorities and areas where you need to direct your energy

- Focus on the goals that align with your purpose.

- Take actionable steps and move forward.

Continue implementing your plan

- Stay committed to consistent progress, even small steps at a time.

- Stay adaptable and open to making adjustments as needed along the way.

Utilize the Learning Log to capture key lessons of your experience on your purpose journey. Refer to Template 8 in the Appendix: Item # → Learning → Action Taken → Key Takeaway.

Learning Log - Template 8

Item #	Learning	Action Taken	Key Takeaway

Learning Log Example

Item #	Learning	Action Taken	Key Takeaway
1	What worked well?	Engaged with other writers; attended conferences for writers and speakers; incorporated book content in speeches, blogs, etc.	Don't be afraid to utilize others in your purpose project. Seek out experts in the field and others on a similar path.
2	What needs to be adjusted?	Table of contents to update to at least ten chapters; Ensure to identify target audience (primary & secondary).	Incorporate project management principles where appropriate. Fine-tuned chapters based on engaging others and receiving input from my crew. Utilize your own experience as a key input into the writing.
3	How can I improve upon the process?	Just write to get my ideas and thoughts on paper.	Do not spend too much time perfecting the product in the initial phases. Revise throughout the process. Seek others who have gone through a similar journey for insight and encouragement.
4	Continually remind me of the Why.	Revisit my purpose of writing this book occasionally	The more time I spent delaying the assignment, the more I tried to talk myself out of the process. Push through when it gets hard.
5	Support others in their journey.	Read and provided feedback to other authors.	Support their work as they fulfill their purpose assignment.

6	This is a big assignment.	Continual prayer for focus and assistance. Focus on the steps and activities to break down the assignment.	If it was meant for me to do, my willingness and divine ability will get me through it.
7	A big part of the book being delayed was my struggle with my faith walk and assignment.	I stayed stuck and delayed writing the book because I did not want to appear evangelistic or preachy. I was unsure if I would turn off the audience or limit my reach.	I had to accept the assignment and be wholeheartedly honest about the intent. I received it from God and could not hide or mask the truth. I live for Him, and whatever purpose and whoever this book is meant for, I believe it will be.
8	Do not view this as a chore.	This is an assignment that is meant for me to do.	I had to incorporate it into my tasks. It had to be prioritized along with my other obligations. It was the only way I could get it done.

Once I accepted my assignment and moved forward, reflecting on the lessons learned and working through the process was the most challenging. I had to continually practice patience and rely on the Lord to overcome hardships. I felt great accomplishment when things were on track, but when it was somewhat derailed, I needed to be reminded of my "Why" and "Who" was ultimately in charge. I, at times, begrudgingly trusted the process.

When faced with the difficulty of implementing a decision you know is right, but it still feels challenging, acknowledge and commend yourself for your extreme courage. Going against the grain and making decisions that align with your true beliefs and values can be tough. Patting yourself on the back reminds you of the strength it takes to follow your convictions, even in the face of adversity. Additionally, being honest with yourself about the difficulty of the situation allows for a genuine acknowledgment of the emotional weight carried in making the right but challenging decision. This honesty can be a source of self-compassion and a reminder that growth often comes with discomfort. Trust in your judgment and allow yourself the grace to navigate the challenges, knowing that your courage in making the right decision is commendable.

The journey toward fulfilling your purpose is not always linear, and facing challenges and setbacks is normal. By reflecting, conducting reviews, and refactoring your approach, you can gain new insights and make necessary adjustments to re-energize and refocus on your purpose-driven plan.

Reflection - _Lake View_

Embracing self-love and acceptance is powerful and allows you to fully appreciate and honor your unique qualities and journey. Expressing gratitude for the purposes and intentions that God has placed in your path shows a deep sense of trust and faith. Remember that you have been given the freedom to choose and decide your actions, and this freedom comes with great responsibility. I love myself and am grateful to just be me. I am thankful for God's purposes and intentions, which were meant for me and placed in my path. I am grateful for the freedom to choose and decide. I am blessed with wisdom and discernment. I am appreciating who I am and what I am meant to do. I will gladly go wherever the Lord leads. I care about those around me. I am thankful for taking well-needed care of myself. I will not compromise on what I need to thrive. I will build and lift others. I am enough. I am Me.

I am thankful to Thee. I am thankful because of She. I am thankful because of He. I am thankful because of We. I am thankful because of Me. I am grateful to Be.

I pray that you find strength and courage in whatever obstacles you face, knowing that God supports you and can overcome them. Let faith be your shield, and perseverance be your companion as you move forward confidently in your purpose assignment.

Proverbs 4: 18 – 19 (NIV)

[18] The path of the righteous is like the morning sun, shining ever brighter till the full light of day. [19] But the way of the wicked is like deep darkness; they do not know what makes them stumble.

NOTES & INSIGHTS:

CHAPTER 7 LAUNCH:
"Go Live"

Launch (Merriam-Webster definition): *To put into operation or set in motion.*

Going live with your purpose is an ongoing process that requires continuous effort, learning, and growth. Stay true to your values and vision and remain open to possibilities. Embarking on this journey signifies your obedience and follow-through and a profound act of entrusting the outcome to the Lord. By this stage in the project, you have surrendered control, understanding that it's not about self-reliance but a transformative shift to selflessness. The responsibility shifts from your shoulders to God.

This chapter is intentionally concise. It does not diminish the value of your efforts but acknowledges that having fulfilled your assignment, you've created space for the Lord to manifest His influence. This surrender is a powerful demonstration of faith and trust, recognizing that, having done your part, your purpose's larger design and fulfillment rest in His hands.

Going live with your purpose assignment is an act of co-creation. It's a realization that while you play an active role in the manifestation of your purpose, there comes a point where you release the need for complete control. This chapter serves as a gentle reminder that you have now positioned yourself to witness the divine orchestration of the rest by completing your assigned project. It's a profound acknowledgment that, beyond your efforts, there is a greater force at play, and your obedience opens the door for the Lord to work through you and bring about the intended impact.

4th Phase: Purpose Go Live

Prepare yourself for whatever the outcome is in this phase. Remember you were chosen to carry out this specific assignment. You are only required to be obedient to the follow-through. Continue to maintain your focus and stay committed to launching your divine plan. Stay connected with your supportive network and consistently pray for guidance and wisdom. You are the best person to complete the assignment and what you were called to do.

This is you *Working on a Project Called LIFE*.

Be sure to prioritize your message and share it with the audience you are directed to. You are blessed with the wisdom to discern how to launch your purpose. Tune into your awareness, and you navigate your path accordingly.

Assess the following considerations and
guidelines as you launch your plan.

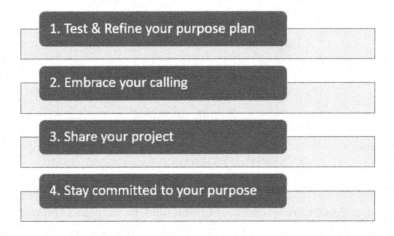

1. Test & Refine your purpose plan

2. Embrace your calling

3. Share your project

4. Stay committed to your purpose

- **Test and Refine**: Consider testing your purpose plan in a smaller setting. This allows you to gather feedback, make necessary adjustments, and refine your approach before scaling up. I utilized my support network by sharing insights from the book with them to see how it resonated. Based on their open and honest feedback, I have made edits using wisdom and understanding. I have also made adjustments utilizing my regular communication channels and my devotions. Remember that you were given this divine assignment, and your plan will come to fruition. This activity is not to redefine your project but to utilize the wisdom and resources you need to launch your plan.

- **Embrace your calling**: Perfection is not the goal when going live with your purpose. You are encouraged to embrace the journey of growth and learning and be willing to take imperfect or even uncomfortable actions. It is better to start and learn along the way than to wait for everything to be perfect. I have chosen to complete the book by the end of the year and plan to self-publish within the first quarter of the following year. I pray for continual insights into the editing and publishing process. I am utilizing wisdom to do the work to welcome what is next.

- **Share your project**: Communicate your purpose and journey authentically with others. Share your story, experiences, and lessons learned to inspire and connect with your audience. Your story can be a powerful tool to attract support and engage others in fulfilling your purpose. Ensure you remain authentic. Tap into your active and authentic listening skills. Additionally, your project's efficient and effective giving will expand your message as you acknowledge that the Lord's will is in process.

- **Stay Committed**: Once you go live with your purpose, stay committed to its continued fulfillment. Be adaptable and willing to adjust your approach based on discernment, feedback, and changing circumstances. Remain focused on your vision and persevere through any challenges and setbacks that you may encounter.

This is your Purpose-filled Project.

From the moment you embraced your calling, this project became an integral part of your journey, alive with purpose and energy. It's a manifestation of your commitment and a dynamic force, continually evolving as you navigate the path of your calling.

Congratulations on your continued journey of purpose, execution, and fulfillment!

Reflection - Ocean View

Be open and willing to go wherever the Lord leads you. Surrender to your calling in implementing your assignment and trust in His divine guidance. Walk confidently, knowing the spirit of fear is not from the Lord. You are valued and have a valuable role to play in the lives of those around you. The ability to build up others and lift them higher is a beautiful act of kindness and compassion. As you lift others, you also uplift yourself and create a positive effect around you.

You are unique and enough, and you deserve to be yourself authentically.

Embrace your true essence and walk confidently in your path.

Stay committed to your purpose, and be patient and compassionate with yourself. Trust in the process, believe in yourself, and keep moving forward with faith and determination.

Proverbs 4: 9 – 11 (NIV)

[9] _She will give you a garland to grace your head;_
and present you with a glorious crown.

[10] _Listen, my son, accept what I say, and the years of your **life** will be many._

[11] _I instruct you in the way of wisdom and lead you along straight paths._

NOTES & INSIGHTS:

CHAPTER 8 WRAP-UP:
"Complete and Close"

Similar to projects, completing and properly closing your assignments are essential to fulfilling God's plan for your life. This phase includes intentional reflection, gratitude, and anticipation for what lies ahead. Neglecting this crucial phase can lead to missed opportunities and a lack of complete fulfillment in your life's purpose. You are encouraged to go back and tie up loose ends, celebrate achievements, and utilize the lessons learned throughout your journey. By concluding your assignments with intention and integrity, you will inspire and encourage those who witness your journey. Your purpose assignment is for your personal growth and the impact you can have on others.

Proper closeout allows you to transition from one assignment to another effectively. As you wrap up completed tasks, you can embrace new opportunities that align with your evolving purpose. Completing your purpose assignment contributes to the legacy you leave behind as well as what you bring forward in support of your divine plan. By intentionally closing each assignment, you will ensure that your impact endures beyond your lifetime, inspiring future generations to pursue their purpose with courage and conviction.

5th Phase: Purpose Fulfillment

You have executed your assigned purpose in Working on Your Project Called LIFE. Throughout the chapters, you have been provided with the tools to embrace and fulfill your assignment.

High-Level Accomplishments (*Refer to Chapter 1*)

- **Confirmed and stated your purpose:**

    o Wrote a clear and concise statement representing your purpose or the specific goal you planned to achieve.

- **Created your objectives:**

    o Broke down your purpose into smaller, measurable objectives.

    o Defined specific and achievable goals that contributed to your overall purpose.

    o Assigned deadlines and target dates to each objective.

- **Developed an Action Plan and identified resources:**

    o Identified the specific actions and steps you needed to take to achieve each objective.

    o Created specific tasks and prioritized them.

    o Listed the internal and external resources available to support your purpose execution.

- **Implemented and adjusted your plan**:

  o Executed your action plan.

  o Regularly reviewed your progress and made adjustments as needed.

  o Monitored and tracked your achievements, noting any challenges or setbacks.

- **Celebrated Milestones**:

  o Acknowledged and celebrated your achievements along the way.

  o Took time to appreciate the progress made towards your purpose.

- **Reflected and learned**:

  o Reflected on your experiences and learned from them.

  o Identified what worked well and what could be improved.

  o Considered any lessons or insights gained during the execution process.

- **Stayed connected and focused**:

  o Stayed connected to your purpose by regularly revisiting and reaffirming it.

  o Maintained focus and motivation through ongoing self-reflection and inspiration.

  o Sought support and encouragement from mentors, friends, and community that shared similar goals.

You are empowered to approach the closing and wrapping up of your purpose assignments with intentionality and purpose, fulfilling God's plan for your life. As I close this assignment by publishing this book, I have received new projects aligning with my writing journey. I am meant to serve, giving of my time and talent. Based on these insights, there are more books to be written.

I celebrate the closeout of your project with you!

While marking its completion, it also stands as a testament to your ongoing obedience, laying the foundation for the execution of future projects that await.

Embrace the anticipation and be prepared for the additional life projects. The future will provide continual opportunities, challenges, and transformative experiences. You have learned that by staying open-minded, cultivating resilience, and nurturing a proactive mindset, you position yourself to welcome and navigate the diverse projects that will continue to unfold on your life's journey. Stay ready to learn, adapt, and grow as you step into the exciting ventures that lie ahead. The future is a realm of possibilities, and your readiness and know-how will shape how you engage with the opportunities that come your way.

Reflection - *Palm Trees View*

Taking a step forward is like a leap of faith, trusting in the path ahead. As I navigate this new chapter of my life, I am filled with a sense of purpose and an unwavering belief that the Lord keeps His promises. The future has already been written, and I have chosen to fulfill my unique purpose.

The diagnosis I received serves as confirmation that my decision to resign from my job was the right one. It validated my obedience in listening to the whispers of my heart and taking the necessary steps to prioritize my well-being. Had I remained in the confines of stress and busyness, I may have dismissed the signs as mere inconveniences, failing to address the underlying problem. I am grateful that I had the wisdom to listen and respond accordingly. Post-surgery, I am feeling renewed and rejuvenated. My headaches have subsided, and I can better do the things I once took for granted. I am easing back into my routine with heightened awareness and caution. I prioritize activities that serve my well-being and contribute to the greater good.

Though thoughts of never-ending costs and finances naturally arise, I firmly believe that if I continue to walk in obedience and trust the process, all my needs will continue to be met. The Lord, my Shepherd, guides me, and I shall not want or lack anything necessary for my journey. Today, the message is more apparent than ever before. I am thankful for this opportunity to deepen my understanding of myself, to grow in faith, and to demonstrate God's will and love through my experiences. I embrace the challenges that lie ahead, knowing that they are part of the larger plan of my purpose. With gratitude and trust in the divine plan, I move forward, knowing that the Lord's provision and guidance will be with me every step.

I am blessed, and I am grateful for the unwavering presence of the Lord in my life. His promises give me strength, and His love fills me with peace. As I continue this journey, I am reminded that my purpose is not for anyone else, but for me to bear and demonstrate. I am chosen, and with each passing day, I am more aligned with my true calling. In the face of uncertainties, I choose faith over fear, trust over doubt, and obedience over hesitation. I surrender my worries and concerns, knowing that the Lord sees me and will provide for me in ways I may not even anticipate. My focus remains on fulfilling my assignment, trusting that in doing so, everything I need will be supplied. I am grateful for the clarity that has emerged and for the Lord's unwavering support. Today and every day, I walk forward with gratitude, faith, and belief, as I am exactly where I need to be.

Proverbs 4: 23 – 27 (NIV)

²³ Keep your heart with all vigilance,
*for from it flow the springs of **life**.*

²⁴ Keep your mouth free of perversity; keep corrupt talk far from your lips.

²⁵ Let your eyes look directly forward,
and your gaze be straight before you.
²⁶ Ponder the path of your feet;
then all your ways will be sure.

²⁷ Do not turn to the right or the left; keep your foot from evil.

NOTES & INSIGHTS:

CHAPTER 9 LET GO: "TAAD"

Hope
Rejected
Deflected
Dejected
Stomped to the ground
Reflected
Accepted
Directed
New and improved

Lisa P-S

Having hope provides the courage and strength needed to persevere in your journey. It rejuvenates the mind and brings encouragement, reminding you that you are not alone. Trusting in the Lord and His plans for you will provide you with protection as you rest in His safety. Hope empowers you to believe in your ability to achieve and take action towards your goals.

As I always say, there is never a dull moment when you are focused and working hard to get things done. Have you ever encountered someone intent on sabotaging your plans and journey? They appear now and then, not fully knowing who you are, but they are presumptuous and seem to know what you need. Stay clear!

This is TAAD - The Anticipated Antagonistic Detractor.

Many TAADs linger around, looking to disrupt your life and calling. You must be ready to remove these detractors and distractions when their bad intentions are exposed. Not everyone's purpose will align with yours or be meant for your benefit. Some individuals are focused on delaying your project. They should be considered issues and managed accordingly. Although expected as a part of life, these occurrences are unwelcome challenges that should not be ignored. As you learned previously, do not get stuck when this occurs. You must stay focused and remain in consistent motion to carry out what you are meant to do.

Let TAAD go. Tune into positivity and tune out negative people and their destructive behavior by practicing a positive attitude and presence, staying productive, and focused on your purpose execution. Learn to love all you encounter, even those not in alignment with you. Ensure you do not let them allow you to lose sight of who you are and what you have been called to do. Practicing a spirit of love will build up defenses against being easily swayed when disappointments and distractions occur.

Leave TAADs behind, and do not let them consume you. Instead, *TURN* your circumstances around by taking back control.

Utilize the TURN principle and:

- **Trust** in your purpose. It is a powerful force that shapes your perspective, fuels your actions, and contributes to a life filled with meaning, impact, and fulfillment. It is a journey of self-discovery and will guide you along the unique path you are meant to walk.

- **Understand** that distractions are a part of life. It is not a resignation to their influence but a strategic acceptance that empowers you to navigate them effectively. This will enable you to be more resilient, adaptable, and mindful in achieving your goals amidst interruptions.

- **Recognize** the need for and importance of keeping your focus. It is not just about avoiding distractions; it's about aligning your efforts with your goals, optimizing your resources, and fostering a mindset that leads to consistent progress and personal fulfillment.

- **Navigate** through the noise to pursue your purpose. This will allow you to maintain clarity, prioritize your goals, and stay focused in the face of distraction.

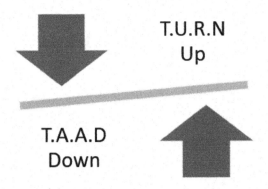

It is crucial to be aware that distractions will come your way. As 1 Peter 5:8 (NIV) reminds us, we should *be alert and sober, knowing that our enemy seeks to disrupt and hinder our progress.* Staying focused and keeping your mind clear and centered is essential for moving forward in the right direction. Don't let distractions limit your time when executing your purpose assignment. Accept the challenge to move out of this state sooner and keep your focus. Stay connected to your purpose and belief. Check-in with your support system, who will encourage and stand by you.

Distractions can set you back but should not be permanent roadblocks.

Because you anticipate encountering risks and issues, you will overcome the obstacles placed in your path to discourage you and take you off course. Don't linger in despair. Stay focused on your purpose and continue making progress on your journey. You were chosen for this assignment. Remind yourself of the calling and assignment you have received. Revisit the initial inspiration and passion that led you to embark on this journey. Reflect on the impact and significance of your purpose to reignite your motivation. Take stock of what you have accomplished so far. Celebrate your achievements, no matter how small they may seem. Recognize the steps you have taken and the growth you have experienced. This reflection can encourage and remind you of your capability to overcome TAAD. It's vital to acknowledge your state. You have been distracted. Embrace this time as a learning opportunity rather than dwelling on it in self-pity. Turn to prayer to seek guidance and ask for divine intervention. Surrender your challenges and concerns to God, asking for wisdom, clarity, and strength. Pray for help in areas where you feel stuck or uncertain. Trust that God will provide the guidance and assistance you need.

TAAD is present because you are doing what you need to do. I remember when I was excelling in my career and was on a trajectory for further growth. Like a blip on the radar, I was assigned a new manager. One who knew nothing about me but saw my credentials, heard the positive feedback, felt challenged, and decided they would limit my growth. It caught me off guard, and I had to take a detour. But that experience solidified that what was meant for me would ultimately be for me. That TAAD encounter inspired me to make myself a priority by intentionally taking control of my growth and personally investing in myself. Since then, I have become more aware of detractors. Do not let them control your narrative. They are not meant to be in your purpose-driven life for the long term; let them go and turn back to what is essential to you.

I was blessed with a solid support network that was there for me on the detour. I rebounded stronger, with a clearer focus. I was also able to be there for some of the same individuals in their TAAD moments/seasons. Stay open and aware of the signs, messages, and opportunities that come your way. Pay attention to the people, resources, and circumstances the Lord may use to provide guidance and insights. Be present in the moment, actively listening, and seeking to discern the next steps. The setback allowed me to step back and give myself a break to refresh my mind and perspective. You are expected to be present and attentive throughout your journey. Check in with yourself. Regularly evaluate and reflect on your progress, challenges, and lessons learned. Adjust your strategies and plans accordingly to stay aligned with your purpose and course correct as needed.

TAADs are common experiences that should not define your journey or purpose. Embrace the process of growth and renewal, trusting that God will guide and equip you to **TURN**, overcome obstacles, and fulfill your assignment.

Common behaviors of TAADers vs TURNers

A Behavioral Checklist

	TAADers	TURNers
A	Attack	Assist
B	Belittle	Build up
C	Criticize	Console
D	Destruct	Design
E	Enrage	Encourage
F	Frustrate	Fortify
G	Get	Give
H	Hinder	Help
I	Interfere	Inspire
J	Jealous	Just
K	Know it all	Knowledgeable
L	Lag	Lead
M	Mock	Motivate
N	Negligent	Nurture
O	Obstruct	Overcome
P	Pitiful	Purposeful
Q	Quitter	Quick-witted
R	Reluctant	Reliable
S	Stifle	Support
T	Torment	Trust
U	Undermine	Uphold
V	Vicious	Validate
W	Wander	Willing
X	Xen*	Xin**
Y	Yucky	Yielding
Z	Zoned out	Zealous

*Xen - Strange or foreign; **Xin - Trustworthiness

<u>Pruning Weeds</u>

Cultivating healthy relationships requires a mindful approach, like tending to a garden containing unwelcomed plants. The dynamic nature of relationships and human connections require continuous assessment and management, similar to the occasional pruning of invasive weeds. It is crucial to evaluate the relationships that need to be nurtured and the ones that may require removal.

In my gardening attempt, I must distinguish between my planted flowers and the unwelcome, overpowering weeds that grew over time. Weeds can appear to add beauty to a space, but if not uprooted, they tend to take over, ultimately covering and damaging the other plants in the area. As I focus on building solid relationships, I evaluate the connections created. I assess those who contribute effectively and ensure I reciprocate with attention and care. Simultaneously, I recognize the destructive influences that are unhealthy and hinder growth. These disrupters are removed. Nurture positive relationships by making space for proper development and growth. Regular 'pruning' or evaluation helps maintain balance and prevents the negative elements from potentially overshadowing the positive. Being intentional and proactive in your relational garden creates an environment where meaningful connections can thrive.

Just as a well-tended garden can transform into a vibrant and flourishing space, active relationship management can lead to a fulfilling and supportive network. Be mindful to tend to the positive, uproot the destructive, ensuring your relationships remain fruitful and fulfilling for solid and lasting connections.

Reflection - _Milestone View_

Living Life

Fifty-plus years of knowledge ingrained, sprinkled with some aches and pains, seasoned with love and growing patience. Giving thanks for being kept through it all. No regrets, not even in the pitfalls. I am forever grateful, thankful, and blessed. Looking forward to what is to come, to be written, to be lived. Giving it all that I've got. One.

Lisa P-S

Throughout this journey, I have encountered fear of the unknown, fear of rejection, fear of success, fear of burnout, fear of validation, fear of exposure, and fear of my abilities and capabilities. I'm not a published author; I was made one through the Lord's guidance. I'm merely an instrument explicitly used to write this book as I live purposefully. I am sure that the outcome will produce a return on the Lord's investment in me. The Lord made the way, and I am focused on following the path.

It's completely normal to experience fear when stepping into the unknown or pursuing something meaningful. But remember that fear should not hold you back from fulfilling your purpose and acting on the guidance you've received from the Lord. You are an instrument used to manifest His plan and bring His message to others. Trust in His guidance and believe He will equip you with the necessary abilities and capabilities to carry out His work.

Fear is often a sign of growth and opportunity. Embrace it as a catalyst for transformation and use it as motivation to step out of your comfort zone. Lean on the Lord's strength and support, knowing He has already paved the way for you. Acknowledging and addressing your fears, can help you confront your fears with courage and determination. Stay focused on your purpose, keep your eyes on the path set before you, and trust that the Lord will provide the resources and support you need. You are not alone in this journey, and the Lord will guide you every step of the way. Walk in faith, knowing that you are fulfilling His plan and making a positive impact through your obedience and actions.

Lord, as I continue to embark on this journey, I seek your guidance and clarity. I pray to remove fears, distractions, and resentments that hold me back. Please provide me with the wisdom to discern your will for my life. I trust you to provide a clear vision and give me the energy and calmness to execute my project to the best of my ability. In Jesus' name, Amen.

Proverbs 4: 14 -17 (NIV)

[14] *Do not set foot on the path of the wicked or walk in the way of evildoers.*
[15] *Avoid it, do not travel on it;*
***turn** from it and go on your way.*
[16] *For they cannot rest until they do evil;*
they are robbed of sleep till they make someone stumble.
[17] *They eat the bread of wickedness and drink the wine of violence.*

NOTES & INSIGHTS:

CHAPTER 10 EPILOGUE:
Have You Encountered Your Purpose?

The Lord encounters each of us differently, at different times, seasons, and phases in our walk with Him. The way we acknowledge these encounters varies. As you explore your spiritual calling, trust yourself and the process. Walking in your purpose is not a one-time event but a continuous journey of growth, service, and discovery. It is important to actively engage in discovering your purpose. You are encouraged and challenged to assess your life, passions, and spiritual calling. Reviewing lessons learned from your journey will give you valuable insights and guidance on identifying and implementing future assignments.

As you encounter your divine purpose, you may be led to act, as you become excited about the potential outcome. Your sense of purpose aligns typically closely with your core values and beliefs. Although it may take you out of your comfort zone, the process consistently reflects your values. Even when things may not make sense from a human perspective, trust that God has a higher purpose and a perfect plan for your life. Surrendering to His guidance and staying connected to your faith will help you navigate unfamiliar territories and uncertainties.

Divine purpose is not selfish. It is often tied to you making a meaningful impact on others. People who have encountered their purpose typically engage in activities that positively affect others and leave a lasting legacy. Those who have found their purpose and are willing to step out in faith are often more resilient in facing challenges. They are committed to their mission and willing to persevere through obstacles.

Encountering one's purpose brings a sense of joy and contentment. It's not just about achievement but also about finding fulfillment in the journey.

Purpose can be deeply spiritual for many individuals. Those who have found their purpose often feel a strong spiritual connection or calling that guides their actions. Purpose usually evolves and expands as individuals grow and change. People who have encountered their purpose are open to continuous growth and development in their chosen path.

Determining if you have encountered your purpose is not always straightforward, but it involves a holistic assessment of your passion, values, impact, resilience, joy, and spiritual alignment. It is an intimate and personal journey that manifests in various ways that are unique to you. As you assess your calling, seek wisdom and discernment through prayer. Stay connected to your identity in Christ and rely on His wisdom to guide your decisions and actions. Being aware of the purposes given to you is a great blessing. It is essential to recognize and value these purposes as they can be a part of a greater assignment that involves other individuals playing their roles. Living a life that aligns with your passions and purposes requires intentional execution.

Living on purpose and executing your known purposes involves taking action, performing, and putting things into motion. Each person's purpose is unique, and even though it may appear as an irregular task, if given to you, it is meant for you specifically. Your assignments may not fit into the usual categories or societal norms, and they might challenge your conventional understanding. Every activity and experience, even if unrelated or unclear, could provide valuable insights into your purpose. Be open to learning from each situation, recognizing that there could be a deeper meaning for your purpose in the process.

For instance, one of my recent assignments was to resign from my job without having another confirmed source of income. This may seem risky or careless from an external perspective, as it deviates from the standard notion of financial stability. Society often judges actions that do not follow the norm as reckless or non-conforming. The need to prove oneself to others can distract you from completing your assignments.

During such times, it becomes crucial to rely on the guidance of the Holy Spirit and move forward as needed. Trusting in God and having faith in the purposes bestowed upon you can provide the strength and clarity necessary to overcome doubts and external pressures. You can fulfill your unique assignments and make a meaningful impact through this alignment with your purpose and spiritual guidance.

Living a life of purpose and executing your assignments requires courage, trust, and a willingness to go against the expectations of others. By embracing your unique path, leaning on your faith, and moving forward with conviction, you can live a life that reflects your purpose and makes a meaningful difference.

Purpose Assignment

Read supporting scriptures:

Jeremiah 29:11 (NIV) "For I know the plans I have for you," declares the LORD, "plans to prosper you and not to harm you, plans to give you hope and a future."

1 Chronicles 28 (NIV): [10] Consider now, for the Lord has chosen you to build a house as the sanctuary. Be strong and do the work. [19] "All this," David said, "I have in writing as a result of the Lord's hand on me, and he enabled me to understand all the details of the plan." [20] David also said to Solomon his son, "Be strong and courageous, and do the work. Do not be afraid or discouraged, for the Lord God, my God, is with you. He will not fail you or forsake you until all the work for the service of the temple of the Lord is finished.

Reflect on it: Consider these verses and the assurance they provide. Consider God's divine plans for you, designed to bring prosperity, hope, and a fulfilling future. Reflect on how these verses resonate with your journey of discovering and fulfilling your purpose.

Put action to it: Write down the plans, dreams, and purposes you believe God has for you. Consider both the big picture and the smaller steps along the way. As you write, allow yourself to dream big and imagine your impact. Then, choose one small action you can take today to move closer to one of those purposes. It could be reaching out to a mentor, researching opportunities, or starting a new project. Take that step in faith and trust that God is guiding you.

Scriptures to support you on your purpose journey

<u>Lead</u>: "Take the Leap"

- Seek God's guidance and direction: **Proverbs 3:5-6** (NIV) – [5] *Trust in the LORD with all your heart and lean not on your own understanding; in all your ways submit to him, and he will make your paths straight.*

<u>Invest</u>: "Set the Stage"

- Seek wisdom and counsel: **Proverbs 15:22** (NIV) – [22] *Plans fail for lack of counsel, but with many advisers, they succeed.*

- Set goals and make a plan: **Proverbs 16:3** (NIV) – [3] *Commit to the LORD whatever you do, and he will establish your plans.*

<u>Focus</u>: "Get in Motion"

- Diligently work on your assignment: **Colossians 3:23** (NIV) – [23] *Whatever you do, work at it with all your heart, as working for the Lord, not for human masters,*

- Seek spiritual growth and maturity: **2 Peter 3:18** (NIV) – [18] *But grow in the grace and knowledge of our Lord and Savior Jesus Christ. To him be the glory both now and forever! Amen.*

<u>Execute</u>: "Follow through"

- Endure trials and challenges: **James 1:2-3** (NIV) – [2] *Consider it pure joy, my brothers and sisters, whenever you face trials of many kinds,* [3] *because you know that the testing of your faith produces perseverance.*

- Seek God's strength in difficult times: **Philippians 4:13** (NIV) – [13] *I can do all this through him who gives me strength.*

Launch: "Go Live"

- Share your message and assignment: **Matthew 28:19-20** (NIV) - [19] *Therefore go and make disciples of all nations, baptizing them in the name of the Father and of the Son and of the Holy Spirit,* [20] *and teaching them to obey everything I have commanded you. And surely I am with you always, to the very end of the age.*

L.I.F.E: "Continued Faithfulness & Purpose Fulfillment"

- Persevere and stay committed to your purpose: **Hebrews 12:1-2** (NIV) - [1] *Therefore, since we are surrounded by such a great cloud of witnesses, let us throw off everything that hinders and the sin that so easily entangles. And let us run with perseverance the race marked out for us,* [2] *fixing our eyes on Jesus, the pioneer, and perfecter of faith. For the joy set before him he endured the cross, scorning its shame, and sat down at the right hand of the throne of God.*

I pray these passages guide and inspire you in your purpose journey. Trust in the word given to you to discern how to apply and execute your specific project or assignment and continue to seek further wisdom and interpretation as needed.

Purpose Filled and Willing

Living purposefully involves having a clear sense of direction, meaning, and significance in your actions and choices. It goes beyond your daily routine and often relates to contributing to something greater than oneself. You may find purpose in various aspects of life, such as relationships, careers, new pursuits, community involvement, or a commitment to personal growth and development. Having a sense of purpose leads to a more fulfilling life. It can provide motivation and a sense of identity.

Willingness is the quality of being prepared or inclined to do something. It involves a readiness and openness to engage with your experiences, challenges, or opportunities. Willingness can be a crucial factor in personal growth and overcoming obstacles. It involves facing discomfort, uncertainty, or fear and being open to what is to come. Willingness can be seen as a practical aspect of pursuing one's purpose. It involves the commitment and action required to achieve your goals and values.

The goal of living a purpose-filled life involves finding meaning and direction, while willingness is about being open and ready to engage with the experiences that arise on that purposeful journey. Combining a sense of purpose with a willingness to embrace challenges can contribute to a more fulfilling and impactful life.

Reflection - *Thankful and Blessed View*

The Lord's love and salvation are ever-present in our lives. He cares deeply about your well-being and has made way for your eternal reward.

As you face challenges and embark on your journey, be comforted, knowing you do not walk alone. The Lord stands with you, providing strength, guidance, and support every step of the way. You will find peace and assurance in your conscious decision to move forward with the right state of mind and in alignment with His will.

Give thanks and praise to the Lord for His mighty works and His faithfulness. He deserves all honor and glory. May your heart be filled with gratitude for His constant presence and the assurance of His salvation. Together, we unite, supporting one another in our respective journeys and celebrating the victories from walking in faith. May the Lord continue to bless and guide you as you fulfill your purpose and live in alignment with His divine plan.

Thank you Lord for your love, grace, and faithfulness. I trust in your mighty power and surrender myself to your will. In Jesus' name, I pray. Amen.

Proverbs 4: 3 – 4 *(NIV)*

³ For I too was a son to my father, still tender and cherished by my mother.
⁴ Then he taught me, and he said to me, "Take hold of my words
*with all your heart; keep my commands, and you will **live**.*

NOTES & INSIGHTS:

TEMPLATES

Template 1: *Purpose Statement*
(Referenced in Chapter 2: Lead - 'Take the Leap')

Item	Insight	Input
Clarity of purpose		
	Assess how well you understand your purpose or the specific impact you want to make.	
	Reflect on whether your purpose is clearly defined and can be articulated concisely.	
Assignment		
	Identify areas where you feel a sense of calling or responsibility.	
	Consider any specific assignments or tasks you believe you have been called or destined to fulfill.	

PURPOSE STATEMENT

Write a clear and concise statement that represents your purpose or specific goal

(At this time, how would you describe the primary purpose and focus of your assignment?)

Template 2: *Purpose Assessment*

(Referenced in Chapter 2: Lead - 'Take the Leap')

Item	Insight	Input
Purpose goals & objectives		
	Set clear goals and define your objectives.	
	Break goals down into smaller, manageable tasks and actionable steps.	
	This activity aims to make the process less overwhelming and enable you to see progress along the way.	
	A clear roadmap will help you stay focused and motivated.	
List To-do's that go beyond day-to-day tasks		
	Identify tasks or activities that align with your long & short-term goals and that support your purpose.	
	Include actions contributing to personal growth, fulfillment, and making a difference.	
List items that appear bigger than you or beyond your reach		
	List goals or dreams that may initially seem challenging or ambitious.	

	Consider opportunities that require stepping out of your comfort zone.	
List what others may have seen in you that you haven't seen		
	Reflect on feedback or observations from others regarding your strengths, talents, and potential.	
	Take note of qualities or abilities that people have recognized in you, but you may not have fully acknowledged.	
What do you spend most of your time on		
	Evaluate where you invest the majority of your time and energy.	
	Determine if these activities align with your core values and long-term aspirations.	
	Identify areas where you feel a sense of calling or responsibility.	

Template 3: *Resource Roster*

(Referenced in Chapter 3- Invest: 'Set the Stage')

Resource Name	Type	Contribution	Commitment	Status

Resource Name: *Name of the resource*

Type: *Kind of resource – people, reference materials*

Contribution: *The role of the resource*

Commitment: *Frequency – i.e., daily, weekly, quarterly, as needed*

Status: *Has the resource been identified, selected, or active?*

Template 4: *Purpose Plan*

(Referenced in Chapter 3 – Invest: 'Set the Stage' &
Chapter 5 – Execute: 'Follow Through')

Activity / Task	Resource	Timeframe (Start / End Date)	Duration (i.e. Days, Weeks, Months)	Status (Not started, in Process, Complete)

Activity / Task: *Action to be taken towards your purpose*

Resource: *The person to perform the action*

Timeframe: *The start and end dates for the action. General time frames, such as quarter/year or month/year, can be used initially. Fine-tune as the plan continues to be developed and the purpose becomes clearer.*

Duration: *The length of time targeted, i.e., days, weeks, months*

Status: *Progress made to date*

Template 5: _Risk Register_

(Referenced in Chapter 3 – Invest: 'Set the Stage')

Risk Description	Action to Resolve	Owner

Risk Description: _Summary of the risk_

Action to Resolve: _What will be done to address the risk?_

Owner: _Who is responsible for addressing the risk?_

Template 6: *Communication Checklist*

(Referenced in Chapter 3 – Invest: 'Set the Stage')

Communication Type	Purpose	Target

Communication Type: *The method of communication.*

Purpose: *The intention of what is being communicated.*

Target: *Who to communicate to?*

Template 7: *Self-Care Schedule*

(Referenced in Chapter 4 – Focus: 'Get in Motion')

Item #	Activity	Action Taken	Frequency

Activity: *What is being done?*

Action Taken: *Detail of what is being done?*

Frequency: *How often (daily, weekly, monthly)? For how long (minutes, hours)*

Template 8: *Learning Log*

(Referenced in Chapter 6 - Learnings: 'Review and Reflect')

Item #	Learning	Action Taken	Key Takeaway

Learning: *The lesson description*

Action Taken: *What was done?*

Key Takeaway: *What lesson was learned, and will it be applied or shared in the future?*

APPENDIX / REFERENCE

- Assign Resources - *Template 3*: Resource Roster with ex.
- *Define Time Blocks - Template 4*: Purpose Plan with ex.
- Additional Planning Considerations
  - *Risk - Template 5*: Risk Register with example
  - *Potential Costs*
  - *Communication - Template 6*: Communication Checklist

o Build Relationships on Purpose
  - Seek Guidance and Mentorship
  - Share your Message
  - Intentional Presence
  - Be a **PAAL (Practice Active and Attentive Listening)**
  - **SHARP** Approach
  - Conscious Connectivity
  - Lifesavers vs Bystanders

o Manage Your Time Purposefully

o Give Back for a greater purpose
  - Effective and Efficient Giving

✿ Side note: Silent Struggles
  o Walk in **STRIDE**

✿ *Reflection* – Shadow View

5. Chapter 4 – Focus: 'Get in Motion'

✿ *Purpose Assignment/Acceptance/Intentional Presence=Focused Purpose*

✿ Get Unstuck
  o Maintain Focus
  o Consistent Motion

✿ Practice Self Care *Template 7*: Self-Care Schedule with example

✿ Prayer

❖ Pruning Weeds

❖ *Reflection* – Milestone View

11. **Chapter 10 – Epilogue: Have you encountered your purpose?**

- o Purpose Assignment
- o Scriptures to support you on your purpose journey
- o Purpose Filled and Willing
- o *Reflection* – Thankful and Blessed View

ACKNOWLEDGMENTS

This heartfelt acknowledgment extends to my day-ones, who have been with me through thick and thin, and also to my current crew, the ones standing beside me in the present moment. You are the actual holders of my ladder, providing unwavering support that extends through the times when I didn't think I could climb any further. Your steadfast presence has been a source of strength, lifting me to complete this project. I am immensely grateful to you.

Special shout out to my hubby, who always allows me to be me. He is truly my *Juan* in multi-millions, and I love him dearly. My children, *Orion* and *Imani*, are my muse and my best self. Although they are a little lazy, they are bright and brilliant! My mother, *Adina* (Lady Di), believes in me and supports me every step of the way. Her prayers and encouraging words kept me focused. The Gayle to my Oprah, my pea in a pod *Tracey,* who has never doubted this day would come. My sissy *Brenda* got me my first introduction to the writing world and the She Speaks conference. My Bahama Mama *Shelley* continually listens and cheers me on. My *BSF* crew has allowed me to grow and open up to fellow believers. I am thankful for you. To the rest of my *Crew,* including my extended family, friends, colleagues, associated organizations, and business partners, I look forward to our continued journey in life on and off the road.

Additionally, to the audience and users of this book, you are the force that breathes life into these pages. Your engagement, dedication to learning and growing, and decision to embark on your journey of self-exploration and development have made this book more than just words on paper. You've transformed it into a living, breathing entity, and I express my deepest gratitude. Your investment in leaping to nurture and groom your journey is a cause for celebration. It reflects a commitment to discovery, growth, and the profound *Project Called LIFE*. It's an honor to share this path with you, and I thank you for choosing to invest in your transformative journey.

As you navigate your assignment and pursue your purpose, I pray for abundant blessings. May your steps be guided, your efforts fruitful, and your impact profound. May the lessons you encounter be wellsprings of wisdom, and may the journey you've embarked upon be a source of joy, fulfillment, and continuous revelation. Here's to you, my cherished readers—thank you for being an integral part of this shared venture, and may your personal life projects be filled with triumphs and remarkable discoveries!

ABOUT THE AUTHOR

Lisa is a vibrant individual, infused with the lively energy of the city and the islands. Her dynamic personality blends urban flair with a down-to-earth and relatable demeanor. Drawing from a wealth of experience, Lisa has demonstrated her leadership prowess by spearheading diverse teams and managing large-scale projects. Her track record is a testament to her versatility, showcasing her ability to navigate and oversee projects across various industries and technologies for over 25 years. Lisa's expertise extends beyond the corporate realm; she has also made impactful contributions to the church ministry, solidifying her leadership skills in faith and community.

Her influence resonates through her professional and spiritual experience, marked by a harmonious blend of sophistication, warmth, and genuine care for people. With a rich history of steering successful endeavors, Lisa brings a seasoned perspective to every project she undertakes, providing both efficiency and a contagious enthusiasm that naturally spreads to the teams she works with.

Her skills include coaching, mentorship, business transformation, project management, portfolio management, relationship management, change management, process improvement, leadership development, training program development, program deployment, and implementation of strategic corporate mandates. She has achieved significant milestones throughout her journey, including successfully managing multi-million-dollar programs, being recognized as an effective leader and connecting teams across multiple generations. Lisa continues to be a force in her assignments, living as a "purpose in progress."

NEXT STEPS

For more information on how I can support your journey, please visit www.Jorions.com to schedule an initial consultation. Jorions LLC is dedicated to helping individuals on their purpose journey and organizations that have chosen to invest in their most important asset, their people. We provide individual leadership coaching and mentoring services. If you're looking for innovative ways to complete tasks, improve team morale, reduce stress, enhance communication, or connect with industry professionals to discuss best practices, our team of experienced consultants are here to help.

With over 30 years of consultation and implementation knowledge across numerous industries, we have the knowledge and experience to help your team perform at its maximum potential. Our focus is on providing customized solutions tailored to your unique needs and challenges. We offer:

- Guidance and mentorship to your team
- Training sessions
- Facilitated team meetings
- Keynote speeches to promote better collaboration and productivity

At Jorions LLC, our success is built on maintaining strong client relationships. We take the time to understand your goals and objectives, working collaboratively to develop solutions that meet your needs and exceed your expectations. *We purposefully prioritize people over process, empowering them to perform at their highest potential.* Visit www.Jorions.com today to start your journey towards improved leadership, team performance, and organizational success.